Salamanders and Newts as a Hobby

by John Coborn

SAVE-OUR-PLANET SERIES

T.F.H. Publications, Inc.
1 T.F.H. Plaza • Third & Union Aves. • Neptune, NJ 07753

Contents

Author's Preface 5

Facts About Tailed
   Amphibians 10

Housing Your Pets 23

Feeding Your Pets 38

Hygiene and General Care 50

Reproduction and
   Captive Breeding 61

Choice of Species 73

Suggested Reading......................97

Index 97

Photography: W. B. Allen, Jr., R. D. Bartlett, W. E. Burgess, J. Coborn, G. Dingerkus, F. J. Dodd, J. Dommers, I. Francais, S. Frank, P. Freed, M. Gilroy, D. Green, B. Kahl, K. D. Kuhnel, K. Lucas, G. Marcuse, S. A. Minton, K. T. Nemuras, A. Norman, E. Radford, P. W. Scott, R. S. Simmons, K. H. Switak, D. Untergasser, L. Wischnath, R. T. Zappalorti.

Inside Front Cover: Jordan's Salamander, *Plethodon jordani.* **Inside Back Cover:** The Marbled Salamander, *Ambystoma opacum.* Both photos by R. T. Zappalorti.

Dedication

For Regina, my daughter.

Distributed in the UNITED STATES to the Pet Trade by T.F.H. Publications, Inc., One T.F.H. Plaza, Neptune City, NJ 07753; distributed in the UNITED STATES to the Bookstore and Library Trade by National Book Network, Inc. 4720 Boston Way, Lanham MD 20706; in CANADA to the Pet Trade by H & L Pet Supplies Inc., 27 Kingston Crescent, Kitchener, Ontario N2B 2T6; Rolf C. Hagen Ltd., 3225 Sartelon Street, Montreal 382 Quebec; in CANADA to the Book Trade by Macmillan of Canada (A Division of Canada Publishing Corporation), 164 Commander Boulevard, Agincourt, Ontario M1S 3C7; in the United Kingdom by T.F.H. Publications, PO Box 15, Waterlooville PO7 6BQ; in AUSTRALIA AND THE SOUTH PACIFIC by T.F.H. (Australia), Pty. Ltd., Box 149, Brookvale 2100 N.S.W., Australia; in NEW ZEALAND by Brooklands Aquarium Ltd. 5 McGiven Drive, New Plymouth, RD1 New Zealand; in Japan by T.F.H. Publications, Japan—Jiro Tsuda, 10-12-3 Ohjidai, Sakura, Chiba 285, Japan; in SOUTH AFRICA by Multipet Pty. Ltd., P.O. Box 35347, Northway, 4065, South Africa. Published by T.F.H. Publications, Inc.
Manufactured in the United States of America by T.F.H. Publications, Inc.

Author's Preface

About 45 years ago, a 5-year-old boy went with his dad to a local pond. In his left hand the boy held a jar by its string handle and in indulged in the same activity—catching newts!

There were two kinds of newts to be had in that pond. The common newt,

his right he proudly sported his first fishing net—consisting of a green netting bag, a wire frame, and a long cane handle. The net had been purchased in a newspaper shop (for some reason in those days newspaper shops always sold fishing nets). On arrival at the pond, there were more dads and small boys also with fishing nets and all were which was called just that—Common Newt or sometimes "Ordinary Newt," *Triturus vulgaris*—and the bigger, scarcer, more colorful and valuable "King Newt"—the Great Crested or Warty Newt, *Triturus cristatus*. The newts were not easy to catch. You had to wait for one to swim into the shallows and then slowly and quietly slide your net

Salamanders in the genus *Aneides*, like the Black Salamander, *Aneides flavipunctatus*, are often called "climbing" salamanders.

beneath it. If you were able to do this, you then made a sudden snatch and pulled

hours of intensive "fishing," the small boy and his dad would return home, the

From a distance, you might easily confuse this California Tiger Salamander, *Ambystoma tigrinum californiense*, with the Spotted Salamander, *Ambystoma maculatum*. They are very similar in appearance.

the net out of the water. Sometimes the newt was much faster than you and you saw it dart away just as you pulled in the net. Other times the newt would somehow mysteriously disappear in the period from when you struck and when you examined the net. Often you would end up with a netful of mud and pondweed, but about one time in ten you would catch a newt, which would then be transferred to a jar of pond water. Of all the newts you caught, only about one in every ten was a "king." After a couple of

proud owners of about 20 ordinary newts and a couple of "kings."

The newts were transferred to an old stoneware sink set into the rock garden in the backyard. The sink had been partially buried in the ground, the plughole had been stopped, and it was filled with water. A few rocks and pondweed had been added to make it more natural, and the newts were fed mainly on worms which the boy would spend hours searching for in the garden. Eventually all the newts vanished; they probably all made their way back to their pond of origin, but the small boy did not know this. He also did not know that a seed had been planted in his mind, for that first newting expedition was the spark that set off a lifetime of interest in animals, especially lower vertebrates.

That small boy was the author of this book; the pond was in Leytonstone, in the eastern suburbs of London, England. The pond has long since disappeared beneath a 20-story block of

In the past, catching and keeping newts and salamanders was considered to be the domain of small boys only, but today such activities may be carried out by both sexes and in all age groups. The attitudes toward our more "creepy" fellow creatures are generally more favorable today than they were at any time in the past. This is probably due to a very real fear and realization that many, even most, of these creatures are on an irreversible decline in

When a member of the genus *Ensatina*, such as this Large-blotched Salamander, *Ensatina eschscholtzi klauberi*, feels threatened, it may stiffen its legs and arch its back and tail. It then looks slightly like a dog "stretching out."

apartments, but it lives on in the memories of all those small boys who caught newts there so many years ago.

population due largely to man's destruction and/or alteration of the environment "for economic gain." Like it or not, we are

Above: Some scientists consider the Swordtail Newt, *Cynops ensicauda*, to be nothing more than a subspecies of the popular Japanese Fire-bellied or Red-bellied Newt, *Cynops pyrrhogaster*. **Facing page:** The Swordtail Newt, *Cynops ensicauda*, gets its species name from the Latin *ensi*, meaning sword, and *cauda*, meaning tail.

witnessing the demise of biological diversity!

The fact that a great many of us are living in towns and cities makes urban man become ever more detached from nature, and leads to a craving for some kind of substitute for the countryside. This often manifests itself in the keeping of some kind of a pet. The word "pet" generally conjures up thoughts of a dog or cat, rabbit or budgerigar, but people are becoming increasingly more interested in the more unusual kinds of "pets." Among these people are those who wish to create a miniature "fauna reserve" in their own home, complete with soil, rocks, plants, and running water, as well as the animals themselves.

This little volume has been written specially for those people who have an interest in the tailed amphibians—the salamanders and the newts—and who wish to learn about the care of these fascinating creatures in the home and/or garden. Additionally, the book will be of some interest to the general naturalists who would like to learn a bit more detail about the creatures around them.

As a person who has been concerned with animals for most of his life both professionally and as a hobbyist, I have always had a soft spot for salamanders and newts ever since my dad took me on that first "fishing" expedition many years ago. If just a small amount of my enthusiasm for these creatures rubs off onto some of its readers, then this book will have served its purpose.

John Coborn
Nanango, Queensland

Facts About Tailed Amphibians

Zoologists currently recognize over 4000 living amphibian species, the vast majority of which are frogs or toads (order Anura). The tailed amphibians, the salamanders and the newts, comprise the order Caudata that contains species will be described in the future.

EVOLUTION OF AMPHIBIANS

The amphibians of today are the modern representatives of those vertebrate (backboned)

Since salamanders and newts belong to the order Caudata, they are frequently referred to as "caudates." Shown here is a rarely seen caudate (at least in the hobby), *Bolitoglossa subpalmata*, from Central America.

about 360 species, or less than 10% of the total number of amphibian species. The complexity of the species and their relationships, however, particularly pertaining to those native to Central and South America and to China, makes it highly probable that further new animals that first colonized dry land many millions of years ago. We can thank the amphibians that we can walk on the surface of the land; they are the ancestors of all the reptiles, the birds, and the mammals, including ourselves. Previous to the amphibian invasion, the land was colonized only by plants and certain insects and spiders. The first vertebrates were fishes that lived in the warm primeval waters. As these primitive fishes evolved into more sophisticated organisms, numerous species

became extinct. Certain groups of fishes, however, developed means of using atmospheric oxygen rather than extracting this essential gas only from the water by means of gills. These fishes eventually developed functional lungs

developed and fierce competion for food and space arose. During this time the topography of the earth was also changing as bodies of water slowly disappeared through evaporation or due to land movements. These changes took place very slowly indeed, over millions of years in fact.

Some of the fish species were better able to tolerate the changes than others, and the latter gradually

and were thus able to spend longer periods in comparatively waterless areas.

It was about 350 million years ago, during a time called the Devonian period, that some of these lung-breathers developed primitive limbs and came out onto the land. The first such land-colonizing pioneers were probably represented by the genus *Eusthenopteron*, which was still a fish but almost an

Hellbenders, of the monotypic genus *Crypto-branchus* in the family Crypto-branchidae, are among the few totally aquatic caudates.

Ensatinas, genus *Ensatina*, lead a completely terrestrial life but rarely stray far from water.

amphibian. In evolutionary terms this was one of the most significant steps in the development of vertebrate life and can be compared with man's current ventures into space.

These land-colonizing fishes soon developed into primitive amphibians, typical of which were those of the genus *Ichthyostega*, which had both fish and amphibian characteristics. The fossil record indicates that the skull of an ichythostegid was about 15 cm (6 in) long and that the total length of the whole animal including its tail was probably about one meter (3 ft, 3 in).

These salamander-like early amphibians showed interesting changes in the proportions of the skull when compared to those of

the fishes from which they evolved: while the portion of skull in front of the eyes was comparatively short and that behind the eyes was comparatively long in the fish, the opposite prevailed in the amphibian, probably partly as a result of the more sophisticated olfactory senses required in the atmosphere. Strong pectoral and pelvic girdles were required by terrestrial amphibians in order to carry their bodies above the surface of the ground. Starting with *Ichthyostega* and its relatives, the evolution of the later amphibians can be conveniently followed.

To change from a water-dwelling organism to a land-dwelling organism was not just a case of developing lungs and limbs; there were other problems to be overcome. Moisture conservation was a major one, and today's modern amphibians still require a moist environment. Those ancient amphibians that led the way in moisture conservation would be the precursors of the lines environment.

Another problem that needed to be solved on the land was the greater influence of the gravity that pulled the body against the earth. Supported by the relatively dense water in which they lived, fishes had evolved a somewhat

that led to the reptiles, the birds, and the mammals. Some amphibians, including salamanders, have managed to develop means of reproducing without the support of open bodies of water, though the majority still must pass a gilled larval stage in an aquatic leisurely system of locomotion through body movements coupled with the steering and stabilizing functions of the fins. The first terrestrial vertebrates, however, required means by which they could raise their bodies and move over an inhospitable surface. A tougher backbone and

Perhaps one of the most underrated salamander genera, at least as far as hobbyists are concerned, is *Bolitoglossa*. Most species are highly attractive and make wonderful pets. Shown here is *Bolitoglossa altamazonica*.

Facing Page:
Although *Not-ophthalmus meridionalis* is in a genus known collectively as the Red-spotted Newts, its common name is the Black-spotted Newt, which goes to show that common names can sometimes be misleading.

more powerful limbs were therefore developed in the earliest stages of their evolution. The hands and arms supported a pectoral girdle that, in turn, supported the front part of the vertebral column. In a similar manner the feet and legs supported a pelvic girdle to perform a similar function at the rear. Thus, the limbs served to support the body against the pull of gravity and also became the means by which the animal could propel itself over the surface of the land. All of the early amphibians retained a tail that functioned as an organ of balance and possibly as a food storage department, but it could still be used as a steering and propelling tool when the creature returned to the water.

These early groups of amphibians radiated into a number of lines depending on the environmental niches that were available. Some of them formed the lines leading to the reptiles, the birds, and the mammals, including ourselves. Some ichthyostegids were probably the forebears of our modern amphibians. They developed first into two distinct groups known as the labyrinthodonts and lepospondyles. Some researchers believe these two groups respectively evolved into the frogs and toads on the one side, and the salamanders and newts on the other. Other zoologists are of the opinion that all modern amphibians arose from a single ancestor rather than having two separate lineages. There is a large gap of geological time separating the labyrinthodonts and the lepospondyles from the modern amphibians; to make things more difficult, intermediate fossil evidence is extremely scarce. How and when the frogs and toads separated from the salamanders and newts is therefore, for the time being, something of a mystery.

CLASSIFICATION

There are millions of different species of living organisms on earth, and as scientists began to catalogue this apparently infinite variety (in the middle of the eighteenth century) it became essential to have a system of classification that was both logical and international. Generations of scientists had already been using classical Latin or Greek to communicate, so it is not surprising that these languages were utilized.

Karl von Linne (1707-1778) was a Swedish naturalist who was also a keen student of Latin. Latinized, his name became Linnaeus. Linnaeus developed the system that was to revolutionize zoological and botanical classification, and he published it in his *Systema Naturae*. In this work he listed all animals and plants known to him at the time and each species was given a double Latin name, the first part being the generic, the second part being the specific. The system was somewhat primitive by today's standards, but methods of diagnosing species characteristics had yet to be developed. Lizards and salamanders, for example, were lumped together in the same group. Over the years, however, Linnaeus's taxonomy has been greatly improved.

As an illustration of the double-name or binomial system of nomenclature, the Rough-skinned Newt of western North America is given the scientific name *Taricha granulosa,* in which the first name is the generic name and the second is the

specific. There are two other species in the genus (*Taricha rivularis* and *Taricha torosa*) and all three show similarities of structure which warrant them being placed in the genus *Taricha*.

Genera (plural of genus) are grouped into greater categories in ascending sequence: family, order,

Order: Caudata (tailed amphibians).

Family: Salamandridae (typical salamanders and newts).

Genus: *Taricha* (western newts).

Species: *Taricha granulosa* (Rough-skinned Newt).

Species sometimes contain an even lower

Although sirens are generally placed in the order Caudata, some scientists once believed they should have their own order, Trachy-stomata. This is a specimen of the Greater Siren, *Siren lacertina.*

class, so on. The following shows how the Rough-skinned Newt is classified.

Kingdom: Animalia (all animals).

Phylum: Chordata (all chordates).

Subphylum: Vertebrata (all vertebrates).

Superclass: Tetrapoda (limbed vertebrates).

Class: Amphibia (all amphibians).

category: the subspecies. A subspecific name is applied to groups of a species that have slight differences, usually as a result of geographic isolation, but with the differences not being sufficient enough to warrant specific rank. In such cases a third name is added to the binomial (making it a trinomial). The Rough-skinned Newt has just two subspecies: the Northern, *T. g. granulosa*, and the Crater Lake, *T. g. mazamae*. The first subspecies to be described has a third name that is always a repeat of the specific name (thus, the Northern Rough-skinned Newt was obviously named first). Genera,

with each other but if they do the resultant offspring usually are infertile hybrids. One of the characteristics of subspecies, however, is that they can and do breed together at the borders of their ranges (if they meet) and produce fertile intergrades that will

species, and subspecies are usually underlined, written in italic script, or in a script different from the main script. Abbreviations may be used in the text after the scientific name has appeared in full once, just as *T. g. granulosa* and *T. g. mazamae* are represented above.

Different species will normally not interbreed

generally show some of the characteristics of both parents. Natural intergrades pose a problem for field researchers where the change over an area from one subspecies to another is gradual; the question posed is often: "at which point does one subspecies become another?" The question of subspecies is a very

A species name is repeated when it is the first in a series of subspecies, as in the case of this Eastern Zigzag Salamander, *Plethodon dorsalis dorsalis*.

controversial one among taxonomists, and beginners are best advised to try and ignore them until they become more knowledgeable.

Scientific names are usually in the style of classical Latin or Greek, as these were the main languages used internationally by scientists at the time of the inception of the binomial system. By learning to use the scientific names of the animals we wish to keep, we can not only overcome the boundaries of language (scientific names being universal), we can also solve the problems derived from a species being called two or more names in the same language. A good example of this is *Triturus cristatus*, which in England may be known commonly as the Great Crested Newt, Crested Newt, Warty Newt, or King Newt, while it has completely different names in other parts of Europe; for example Triton a crete (French), Kammolch (German), Kamsalamander or Grote Watersalamander (Dutch), Storre vattensalamander (Swedish), Tritone crestato (Italian), Traszka gorsca (Polish), Colek velky (Czech) and Gryebyenchatski triton (Russian).

UNDERSTANDING SALAMANDERS AND NEWTS

Many people are familiar with the life cycle of a typical frog. For some reason or other, the frog seems to be a much more popular subject for school biology lessons than the salamander or the newt. If we wish to keep our tailed amphibians in optimum conditions, however, it is important that we are reasonably familiar with their biology and habits, especially if we hope to breed them.

Newt or Salamander?

There is no real scientific

difference between a newt and a salamander; the two words are really colloquialisms describing different types of salamander, and another good reason for the use of scientific nomenclature. Generally, however, the term "salamander" may be applied to any tailed amphibian but "newt" is usually applied to those species that are terrestrial from late summer through winter but become aquatic in the spring for the purpose of reproduction. Male newts often have elaborate seasonal courtship dress and breeding behavior with which to impress their prospective mates. Newts are represented in Europe and North Africa mainly by the genus *Triturus*, in Asia by the genera *Cynops*, *Paramesotriton*, *Tylototriton*, and others, and in North America by the genera *Notophthalmus* and *Taricha*.

The order Caudata comprises some 360 species of tailed amphibians in nine families native to North and South America, Europe and North Africa, and Asia, predominantly in the northern temperate and

Sometimes animals are named after people. In *Cynops ensicauda popei*, for example, the subspecies name honors noted herpetologist Clifford H. Pope.

colder zones. They are totally absent from Australasia and do not occur in tropical parts of Asia and Africa or southern temperate areas.

A typical salamander has soft, moist skin; an elongate body; and a well-developed tail often as long as or longer than the body. The neck is more or less distinct from the head and body, and the shape superficially resembles that of a lizard (for which the salamander is often mistaken) though there are some species that have reduced limbs and a few (sirens) in which the rear limbs are absent. In spite of the lizard-like appearance, closer examination of a salamander will reveal no scales, no claws, and no external ear openings, all possessed by typical reptiles. The eyes are relatively small but functional and usually distinct, with or without movable eyelids. The larynx is poorly developed and, unlike the Anura (frogs and toads), there is usually no voice, but a few species can emit a sort of protest "squeak" if threatened. With the exception of the Plethodontidae, which are lungless, the left lung is smaller than the right but still functional.

Most salamanders and their larvae are carnivorous (though the sirens may be partially herbivorous). The smaller species feed on small insects, crustaceans, worms, molluscs, etc., while some of the larger ones will take any small vertebrates or invertebrates they can overpower, including fish, frogs, and other salamanders, as well as carrion.

The majority of the tailed amphibians are nocturnal and very secretive in their habits; in fact, the average person rarely sees one in the wild unless he knows what he's looking for. Caudates may be totally terrestrial, totally aquatic, or semi-aquatic, depending on the species.

During its terrestrial stage, the Marbled Newt, *Triturus marmoratus*, has a rounded tail. During its aquatic stage, however, the tail is flattened from side to side and acts like a rudder.

The larval stage of the Spring Salamander, *Gyrinophilus porphyriticus*, is particularly long, sometimes lasting up to three years.

In a few cases, the climate will dictate whether the species are aquatic or terrestrial at any particular time.

Breeding behavior exhibited by the various species ranges from simple meet and mate tactics to elaborate courtship rituals (the latter is particularly applicable to newts of the genus *Triturus*). In most cases fertilization is internal, but accomplished without copulation. The male deposits a gelatinous, pyramidal structure, the spermatophore, on the substrate. This spermatophore is capped by a capsule of spermatozoa and the whole object is retrieved by a receptive female with her cloacal lips. The spermatophore dissolves in the female's body but the spermatozoa are stored for later use. As the eggs are laid, they are fertilized by individual sperm cells.

An exception to the above rule is the reproductive behavior exhibited by members of the family Cryptobranchidae: the East Asian Giant Salamanders (*Andrias*) and the North American Hellbender (*Cryptobranchus*). In these species the females first lay the eggs and these are sprayed with milt by the male, much in the manner of most fish species.

Most salamanders lay their eggs in water, but there are some exceptions, especially among the plethodontid salamanders. The eggs are generally deposited individually and attached to the foliage of aquatic vegetation or debris. The egg has a thin coating of a substance that

Members of the genus *Pseudo-eurycea* guard their egg clutches until the young have completely metamor-phosed within the egg. Shown here is *Pseudo-eurycea gigantea.*

reacts with the water to form a thick, protective, gelatinous layer.

In most species the eggs hatch as aquatic, gilled larvae that require a period of time in water in order to gradually metamorphose into adults. These larvae begin to feed upon tiny aquatic animals within hours of hatching. Unlike the tadpoles of frogs, the larvae have conspicuous, feathery, external gills on either side of the head, and the front limbs develop before the rear (opposite in frogs).

In some species, the eggs develop to various stages inside the female's body and may eventually be deposited directly into the water. In a few species, complete metamorphosis takes place within the maternal body and fully formed miniature versions of the parents are eventually born on dry land. Many woodland salamander species do not require water in which to lay their eggs, but deposit them in some suitably moist cavity, perhaps in a hollow log or under a rock. The larvae develop within the eggs and hatch as small versions of the adults.

Housing Your Pets

All animals kept in captivity rely entirely on their owner for their welfare and should be treated with the greatest of respect. The first considerations for the prospective salamander or newt keeper must be planning the accommodations required well in advance; it is not a very good idea to acquire the animals first and then start worrying about housing them. It is recommended that each species be kept in a separate accommodation, not only so that differences in habitat or habit can be catered for, but because some species are unable to withstand the body secretions of others. In addition, some species will not only eat other species almost as large as themselves, they may even eat their own siblings.

A tank in which small animals are kept may be called an aquarium, a terrarium, or an aqua-terrarium. An aquarium is used for keeping species that are totally aquatic, while a terrrarium is for terrestrial (land-dwelling) species. There may be uses for both of these types of accommodations in your home, but by far the greatest number of pet caudates require an aqua-terrarium. These are for species that are amphibious and require water in which to breed.

In addition to knowing whether your chosen species is terrestrial, aquatic, or semi-aquatic, you should know something about its habits

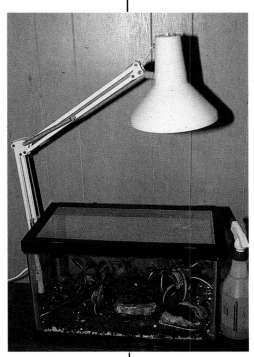

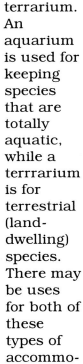

Salamander terraria need not be elaborate. An inch or so of soft moist soil and a few plants will do fine for many terrestrial species.

Since ensatinas, genus *Ensatina*, are for the most part terrestrial, you need to supply them with only a small water bowl.

and native habitat so that it can be supplied conditions as near to natural as possible.

The Aquarium: An aquarium is a tank for totally aquatic species (Axolotls or amphiumas, for example) where no land area is required. Several kinds of aquarium tanks may be available at your local pet store, ranging from the traditional steel-framed glass tanks (now largely obsolete but you might come across one from time to time) to clear plastic and all-glass tanks. All-glass aquaria are the most commonly used today and are recommended as display tanks—cheaper plastic tanks or even goldfish bowls can be used for breeding, rearing, quarantine, etc. The all-glass tank consists of glass panels cemented together along the edges with a special silicone sealant. Such aquaria can be purchased ready-made; you could have one built to your specifications or you could quite easily make one yourself.

Tank dimensions will depend on the number and size of the animals you wish to keep, but if you work to a minimum size of 60 cm long by 30 cm wide by 30 cm deep (2 ft x 1 ft x 1 ft) you will not go wrong. Such a size would be perfectly suitable for a pair of Axolotls. Bear in mind that a tank containing water is rather heavy; in the size mentioned above the water alone will weigh 54 kg (approximately 120 lbs or over 1 cwt.) and to this we have to add the weight of the tank itself plus the substrate and decoration materials (gravel and rocks are even heavier than water). Ensure therefore that the base and stand on which the tank is kept are very sturdy and preferably reinforced with angle irons.

As far as substrates are concerned, it is good to create an environment in the tank that is as natural-looking as possible. Try and picture the sort of environment in which your chosen species lives in the wild. Although for various reasons it will not be possible to recreate the environment exactly, we can use compromise solutions in many cases. For example, many aquatic species live in watercourses with thick muddy bottoms, something that is extremely difficult to duplicate attractively in the aquarium. We can, however, substitute the mud with clean, fine gravel, without any detrimental effect to the animals. The aquascape for aquatic salamanders or newts is similar to that of an ornamental fish tank and you will obtain many interesting tips from books about tropical or cold-water fishkeeping.

The best substrate is a layer of washed aquarium gravel about 5 cm (2 in) deep at the front, sloping up to 7.5 cm (3 in) at the rear (deeper for larger tanks) of the tank. A few non-toxic rocks or river pebbles (granite, slate, etc., although limestone should be avoided) are used for decoration and placed to form caves, valleys, and terraces. Treated bogwood can be purchased at aquarists suppliers and is very decorative. If you try and grow aquatic plants together with most of the larger aquatic salamanders you will usually be fighting a losing battle as the continual grubbing actions of the animals will just uproot them. The best method is to use only robust plants which are allowed to develop a stable root system before the animals are introduced.

The Aqua-terrarium: Most salamander species require an aqua-terrarium with a varying ratio of land

For most aquatic species, a setup complete with plenty of plants will be greatly appreciated.

to water depending on the species being kept (although in most cases roughly half land and half water will be adequate). An aqua-terrarium is also ideal for breeding many species and is especially useful for rearing larvae to their terrestrial stage. An all-glass aquarium tank can be used, with the addition of a glass partition about 15 cm (6 in) high cemented (with the silicone sealant) across the bottom of the tank to make a waterproof barrier between the land and the water. The water area can be given a 2.5 cm- (1 in-) thick layer of fine grade aquarium gravel, thus giving a water depth of 12.5 cm (5 in). To provide easy exit from the water, a gradient of rocks and pebbles can be placed up the side of the glass partition.

The land area is half filled with stones and coarse gravel to provide drainage (ideally a drainage hole should be incorporated into the floor of this area), then a mixture of sterilized garden loam, peat, and coarse sand (commercial potting mix is ideal) is placed on top to fill in the area and slope up and away from the

water. A slab of turf or pieces of moss may be placed over this, coupled with mossy bark or stones to form hiding places. Plants are preferably left in their pots so that they can be changed easily (it is often difficult to get plants to fare well in a terrarium, so keep two sets of plants

so that they can be given regular periods of "rest and recreation"). The pots can be sunk into the substrate or concealed behind rocks, bark, etc. If possible, use plants which are compatible with the conditions in the tank, and for authenticity try and get plant species which come from the same part of the world as your salamanders.

If you are ambitious enough (and can afford it), it is possible to construct a built-in aqua-terrarium in an alcove of your house or conservatory. Such a display can have a concrete, fiberglass, or plastic pond, waterfalls,

built-in sprinklers, etc. The back wall of the display can be built up with mossy rocks, and cavities between them can be filled with potting compost to take lush, moisture-loving plants. The whole unit is enclosed behind framed glass doors, with fine mesh (insect screening) panels above for ventilation. With careful and artistic planning you can create an attractive, natural-looking indoor section of woodland in which your salamanders and/or newts really feel at home and will be more likely to reproduce without any problems.

The Terrarium: A container constructed for species that are totally or almost totally terrestrial and which do not require large volumes of water in which to breed (some plethodontid salamanders, for example) is a terrarium. A box-like timber construction with a glass viewing panel in the front may be used, but since high humidity is required, a better option would be a tank made entirely of glass or a mixture of glass and acrylic sheeting (plexiglass). The advantages of using acrylic sheeting in one or more of the sides are that it can easily be drilled and shaped and is an ideal material for sliding ventilation panels (affixed on one or more sides). The main panels should be of high quality glass so clear viewing is possible.

Ideal dimensions for a group of say, 6

Some salamanders have both a terrestrial and an aquatic stage. Captives in the aquatic stage must of course be given an appropriate tank such as the one this Northwestern Salamander, *Ambystoma gracile*, is in.

plethodontids would be 75 x 50 x 50 cm tall (30 x 20 x 20 in). The substrate would consist of a layer of clean gravel covered with slabs of living moss (which may have to be changed regularly). A couple of potted ferns, the pots disguised by bark or rocks, and a piece of rotting log decorated with living

One advantage to having many plants in a salamander tank is that it gives them more places to hide. They will take such opportunities with great eagerness.

epiphytic plants will provide attractive furnishings. Additionally, or alternatively, a potted creeping plant can be used to provide extra interest and cover for the salamanders.

LIFE SUPPORT SYSTEMS

The important additional life support systems in the aquarium or terrarium include temperature control, lighting, ventilation, and humidity.

Let us examine each of these items individually.

Heating

Salamanders and newts require various ambient temperature levels, depending on where they originate. The majority of captive species come from warm- to cold-temperate climates, so supplementary heating is not normally required, particularly if the animals are kept indoors. Should you live in a cold climate and wish to keep sub-tropical or tropical species, then your terrarium will naturally require supplementary heating in order to maintain optimum temperatures for the species in question. On the contrary, some of the temperate and cold-weather species may require cooling if kept in warmer climates. If you keep species native to the area in which you live, however, then you probably will not require any special warming or cooling facilities.

The most satisfactory means of heating a terrarium probably is to use the aquarium heaters that are normally supplied for tropical fish tanks. There are numerous brands, sizes, and strengths available from specialist dealers, but most consist of a heating element and a thermostat housed in a toughened glass tube and a waterproof stopper through which the power cable passes. The thermostat may be easily adjusted to the required temperature. The heater is simply placed in the water of the aquarium or aqua-terrarium. In the latter, the heater will also raise the temperature of the air space as well as maintain high humidity. In the dry terrarium, the heater simply can be placed in a concealed container (a clean pickle jar or similar) of water where it will act as a heater and humidifier.

The ordinary domestic light bulb was once the standard form of heating for a small terrarium, and in spite of improvements in heating technology, these lamps still have their uses. They are cheap, come in various sizes, and by experimenting with various wattages you will be able to come up with the desired

The Tennessee Cave Salamander, *Gyrinophilus palleucus*, is indeed a fascinating caudate, but it is rarely seen in captivity outside of science labs.

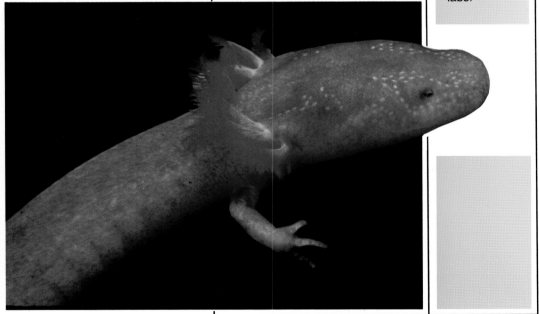

The Fire Salamander, *Salamandra salamandra*, is a very popular pet species, probably due to the fact that it doesn't need much beyond some moist soil, a small water bowl, and a few crickets on feeding day.

temperature. A disadvantage of these lamps is that that warm-weather species requiring warmth at night will be inflicted with "continuous daylight." If you require the bulb to light the terrarium during the day and still have warmth at night without too much light, the answer is to have two bulbs—a clear one for daytime and a dark-colored one (red and blue are the best colors) for nighttime, the latter being of a smaller wattage so you can create a cooler nighttime temperature simultaneously.

Be cautious about using the high-wattage, infra-red heat lamps that are favored by many reptile keepers. When used, such a lamp should be suspended above the tank and the beam directed through the gauze or mesh of the lid. An optimum temperature can be achieved by experimentally moving the lamp up or down, but it is best to do this without animals or plants in the tank until you have got it right. For most salamander and newt species, heat lamps are not really necessary and it is barely worth the risk of using them.

Another form of heating that may be considered is the heating cable or heating pad of the type used by horticulturists to provide "bottom heat" for their plants. The cable can be coiled through the substrate and the pad placed under the terrarium.

Like all amphibians, the caudates are ectothermic and maintain their

preferred body temperature by moving among a range of external temperatures (this applies mainly to terrestrial species or species during their terrestrial stage rather than aquatic species whose constant temperatures are more usual). The preferred body temperature varies from species to species and will be influenced by the climate of its native habitat. In order to let captive amphibians adjust to their own preferred body temperatures in the terrarium, a range of temperatures can be provided. This can be done by placing the heating apparatus at one end of the terrarium only; the warmest area will then be near the heater and the temperature will reduce gradually with the distance away from it. The animals will then be able to select a spot to rest where they feel most comfortable.

A nighttime drop in temperature is normal in most climatic zones; the temperature variance may be as little as 3°C (4.5°F) in low altitude equatorial areas, but can be as much as 20°C (36°F) or more in continental, temperate, or montane climates. Most caudates will appreciate a temperature reduction of 5 to 10°C (9 to 18°F) at night, and this can be achieved simply by turning the heater off each evening and on again each morning (which is when an electric timer will come in handy). In the average house, the prevailing room temperature is adequate for most salamanders and newts at night.

Since the Mountain Dusky Salamander, *Desmognathus ochrophaeus*, occurs primarily in the higher elevations of the eastern United States, it need not be kept in particularly warm surroundings. An ambient temperature of 65°F (18°C) is sufficient.

Gravel is an acceptable substrate for aquatic salamander and newt species, but for terrestrial caudates you will need something a little softer since they will very likely burrow into it.

Variations of seasonal temperatures must also be taken into consideration. Reproductive cycles in most species are influenced one way or another by seasonal climatic changes, and many species require a winter temperature reduction if breeding is to be successful.

Lighting

Although most tailed amphibians are nocturnal and very secretive, this does not mean that lighting should be ignored in their terraria. The biorhythms of salamanders and newts are affected by photoperiod (daily duration of light), and many species rest during the day and are stimulated into action as the sun goes down. Outside the tropics, seasonal changes of photoperiod are also a great influence, and the reproductive activities of temperate species are triggered by a combination of increasing photoperiod of daylight and a gradual temperature increase.

The most successful captive breeding occurs when amphibian species are offered a dark/light cycle similar to that of their native habitat. Should more than one compatible species be kept in the same terrarium, try and choose species that come from similar habitats and climatic areas. Artificial lighting is most appropriate in indoor terraria as natural sunlight entering through glass will soon produce lethal temperatures unless the greatest of care is taken.

Of course, if you decorate your terraria with living plants, suitable lighting is even more important and it is essential that the artificial light source you use is of the highest quality. Continuing research into "artificial daylight"-type lamps is producing ever-improving systems. Horticultural lamps and fluorescent tubes which emit a quality of light ideal for indoor plant growth are now available. The lamps come in all sorts of sizes, shapes, and wattages, so you should be able to find something suitable for every type of terrarium. It is a good idea to obtain a manufacturer's description of the various types available and give it a good read before deciding what is the best type of lighting to suit your own situation. Most fluorescent lamps can be mounted in brackets in the aquarium lid. Lamps that emit a great deal of heat with their strong light (quartz-halogen for example) should be placed well above the terrarium (you will have to experiment with a thermometer to work out how far above) and have their beam directed through a gauze or mesh screen.

Humidity and Ventilation

It is very important to arrive at a compromise

The Spotted Salamander, *Ambystoma maculatum*, is a very hardy captive, taking crickets and other small insects. The specimen shown here, incidentally, is quite unusual—it has almost no spots.

Many of the salamanders in the family Ambystom-atidae make fine pets, but some of them, like this Flatwoods Salamander, *Ambystoma cingulatum*, may be hard to find on the pet market.

humidity and ventilation situation in a terrarium containing amphibians. The problem is that if you have high humidity without ventilation, the air in the terrarium will soon become foul, and molds will develop on the substrate, bacteria will flourish, and your animals will be subject to disease. Conversely, over-ventilation will cause the air to dry out very quickly, posing another danger to your moist-skinned amphibians. Adequate ventilation will prevent a build-up of foul, organism-laden air and remove excess carbon dioxide, while adequate humidity will ensure that your amphibians and plants flourish.

All terraria should have ventilation grills fairly low down on the sides and also in the lid; this will allow a constant air exchange in the container. An aquarium heater in the water will create convection currents and speed up ventilation. An aerator in the water will also provide additional ventilation as well as improve the humidity in the air. Humidity can also be increased by regular (at

least twice a day) mist spraying. Living plants will themselves help to keep the humidity high, as well as contribute to keeping the air fresh.

Filtration

Most aquatic and semi-aquatic caudates can be considered rather messy. Though this is all part of the natural cycle in the wild, they will soon pollute the water in the relatively small volume of water in the aquarium or aqua-terrarium. The water will thus either have to be changed frequently, or you can install a filter. Since it is not advisable to disturb your animals too frequently, it is better to take the latter course. A simple and inexpensive but reasonably efficient box filter is operated by an air pump. Such a filter consists of a plastic (usually) box loosely packed with an inert filter medium such as nylon wool. The filter works on the principle that rising air bubbles create an upward current in the water. An air line, with a small airstone attached, is run to the bottom of the tube in the center of the filter. The rising air bubbles (research has shown that medium-sized bubbles create a better current than either large or very small bubbles) will create a current up the tube, causing the replacement water from the body of the tank to continually flow through the filter medium where suspended materials accumulate. The filter

Filtration is an essential consideration when housing an aquatic salamander like the Broken-striped Newt, *Notophthalmus viridescens dorsalis*. This of course holds true for fully aquatic species as well.

Since the Large-blotched Ensatina, *Ensatina eschscholtzi klauberi*, spends the majority of its time on land, keeping one in a greenhouse is a perfectly feasible idea. You should, however, still provide some type of aquatic area.

medium is fairly easy to wash or change at regular intervals. Such a filter is quite adequate for small volumes of water, especially if say, at weekly intervals, part of the water is changed (for example: remove a jugful and replace it with a similar amount—this provides much less disturbance than completely replacing all of

the water every few days).

It is advisable to use a power filter for larger volumes of water. A power filter consists of a relatively large, electrically driven pump that forces water through a filter chamber before returning it to the tank. There are many commercial types manufactured primarily for fish-keepers. Your pet shop or aquarist suppliers will be able to give you information and advice on

the use of power filters and suggest what is the best for your needs.

THE GREENHOUSE

Salamanders and newts can be kept in a greenhouse, even those species from sub-tropical or tropical climates, as long as you are able to maintain adequate temperatures throughout the year and

remember that you only need a power failure for a few hours in the winter and all your efforts may be lost (it is well worth investing in an emergency heating system if you ever intend to go into tropical salamander breeding).

However, there are some great advantages in keeping your animals in a greenhouse. They will, for example, be able to breed in almost natural conditions if you provide

A true challenge for the keeper is the Eastern Newt, *Notophthalmus viridescens*. It starts out as an aquatic larva, then becomes terrestrial (when it becomes known as a "Red Eft," shown here), then returns to an aquatic life during its sexually mature years.

them with the right facilities. Water tanks or artificial ponds can be let into the floor of the greenhouse for species that require deep water or relatively large surface areas in order to breed (beware of overheating in the summer—you should have adequate ventilation). To prevent the inmates from escaping, all windows and other ventilation openings should be covered with insect screening.

THE OUTDOOR ENCLOSURE

A most satisfactory method of keeping native amphibians and those from a similar climate to that where you live is in an outdoor pond or enclosure. Once you have built a pond, constructed a wall around it (preferably with an overhang at the top to prevent escapes), and landscaped the land area, you have little else to do since the animals will virtually look after themselves. They will find most of their own food, though it will do no harm to feed them individually at regular intervals with a few mealworms or maggots. Good breeding results are frequently reported by owners of such outdoor enclosures as, in most cases, the animals are hardly aware that they are in confinement.

Feeding Your Pets

Most members of the genus *Bolitoglossa* can be fed on earthworms and small insects. Shown is *Bolitoglossa subpalmata*.

All kinds of animals, whether they are cats, dogs, cockatoos, ants, elephants, crocodiles, humans, or salamanders, require a balanced diet if they are to stay in the best of health and function properly. A balanced diet is one that contains the basic nutrients (proteins,

in the case of some of the larger species, small vertebrates. By consuming a variety of prey, an animal gets all its requirements. There is a possibility that the undigested vegetable contents of the stomachs of herbivorous creatures consumed by salamanders will also have beneficial

carbohydrates, fats), vitamins, and minerals in a ratio suitable for the animal in question. Animals acquire their basic nutrients by eating a variety of foods, but most salamander and newt species are almost totally carnivorous, feeding on a variety of invertebrates or,

effects on the salamander.

Obtaining an adequate supply and variety of food items can be a difficult aspect of your hobby. Most salamanders consume only livefoods and it is the movement of the prey that usually influences the amphibian to catch it (aquatic species, however, often rely on the senses of touch and smell to find prey; this explains why they will take carrion in the wild or strips of meat in

COLLECTING FOODS

Due to the availability of commercial livefoods, collection from the wild is perhaps not resorted to so

captivity). Today, the terrarium keeper is fortunate in having access to several species of commercially raised invertebrates suitable as food for amphibians and other insectivorous animals. You could also start your own cultures of various prey animals. This will save you money as well as provide you with permanent supply of foodstuffs.

much today as it was in the past. However, it is highly recommended that your salamanders and newts be fed at least partially with collected food as this is bound to introduce nutrients into the diet that would otherwise not be available. The extra variety will also help relieve the "boredom" which can arise from a monotonous supply of two or three varieties of cultured

In captivity, the Red Eft (the terrestrial stage of the Eastern Newt, *Notophthalmus viridescens*) will eat standard caudate foods such as small insects.

foodstuffs.

Perhaps the best means of collecting a variety of terrestrial insects and spiders (sometimes quaintly called "meadow plankton") is to use a canvas-reinforced sweep-net. The mouth of the net is simply swept through the foliage of tall grasses, weeds, trees, and shrubs. The small insects and spiders caught in the net are then transferred to plastic or glass jars or food storage boxes for transport home. A great variety of caterpillars, moths, beetles, bugs, grasshoppers, spiders, and so on can be collected in this way. These insects are best graded into suitable sizes and will then be eagerly taken by your salamanders. It is advisable

not to overfeed with insects at any one time; allow one lot to be devoured before introducing the next or you are likely to get escapees in your house. Excess insects are also likely to drown in the salamander's water supply and pollute it.

A variety of invertebrates can often be found by turning over rocks, logs, and other ground debris. Here you will certainly capture a selection of pill bugs, beetles, earthworms, slugs, and snails. Many small insects congregate in flower heads; these are very suitable for small salamander species and newly metamorphosed youngsters. Collect such insects with a tool called a "pooter." A pooter is a glass or plastic bottle with a cork through which two glass tubes are passed. One tube, the mouthpiece, is bent over at right angles and passes just through the cork; the other tube is straight but extends almost to the base of the bottle. A piece of flexible rubber tubing is attached to its outer end. The end of this tubing is placed close to the insects in the flower heads and they are captured by sucking sharply on the mouthpiece. The insects will be drawn through the glass tube into the bottle. A piece of wadding placed in the mouthpiece will prevent you from accidentally sucking up any insects.

Large numbers of ants or termites can be collected quite easily. Though the former are rejected by most salamanders (due to the formic acid taste), there are some species (some plethodontids, for example) that are specialized ant eaters. However,

most terrestrial salamanders will eagerly take termites, a particularly nutritious contribution to their diet. If you are lucky enough (or maybe unlucky depending on your point of view) to live where there are termite nests, you can simply chip a small piece of the mound away at regular intervals and place it complete with the termites in the terrarium. The nest will be quickly repaired by the termites left in residence, leaving you with an almost constant food supply for your salamanders.

Although the most difficult aspect of keeping a Georgia Blind Salamander, *Haideotriton wallacei*, is probably maintaining its surrounding temperature, feeding it is quite easy. It will eat bloodworms, tubifex, and shrimp.

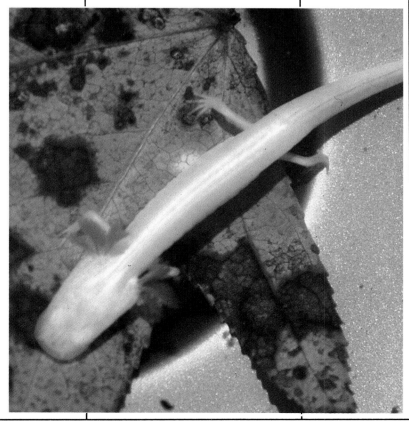

Dragonfly nymphs are not a good meal for most salamander and newt species. They can be aggressive and may actually harm your pets.

Aphids (commonly called greenflies or blackflies) are a good and convenient food item for very small terrestrial salamanders. Aphids congregate in large numbers on the growing tips of many plants (especially cultivated ones). If you cut off a plant tip complete with aphids and place it in the terrarium you will find that the insects will soon sense something is wrong and start wandering about, only to be snapped up by your salamanders.

A flytrap can be a useful asset to the home terrarium keeper; there are several types available on the market. Alternatively you may want to try making your own; it is quite easy. Insect screening mesh placed over a wire or timber frame mounted on a flat board (about 30 cm—1 ft square) is adequate. The board should have a 1 cm (½ in)-diameter hole in the center, over which a plastic funnel is inverted. The board is placed on four blocks so that there is adequate space beneath. Flies will be attracted to any smelly meat or fish that you place under the board (an additional asset is the side-production of maggots). If alarmed, or after feeding, the flies will make for the strongest source of light, which is the

hole in the board directly above them. They will then make their way through the funnel and be trapped in the mesh cage. In order to remove flies, you can have a knotted muslin "sleeve" set into one side of the cage. You can undo the knot and insert your hand with a jar to collect flies.

Aquatic salamanders and carnivorous larvae require free-swimming livefood. Various freshwater crustaceans, ranging from the tiny *Cyclops* and *Daphnia* to the relatively large freshwater shrimps and crayfish, can be netted or found by turning over rocks near the edges of streams, creeks, etc. The larvae of many flying insects (mosquitos, mayflies, etc.) are aquatic and are also excellent food for some salamanders. When collecting aquatic livefoods, be careful not to introduce voracious larvae such as those of dragonflies or water beetles, which could regard your salamanders as an item for the menu!

CULTURED LIVEFOODS

Though preferable, it is not always possible to provide your salamanders with collected livefood all the time. Maybe you do not have time for collecting (especially if you live in the

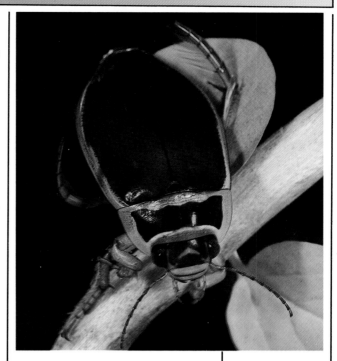

city and would have to travel out into the country). In the winter there is not much livefood to be found anyway, though if your salamanders are hibernating you will have no problem. Whatever your situation, it is advisable to have a standby supply of cultured livefoods, or at least find out where you can get them if an emergency should arise. Though many hobbyists prefer to culture their own livefood, there is really no need to if you can't tolerate the hassle. Various livefoods are cultivated commercially and you can simply buy them at your local pet shop or get a regular small supply of

Like dragonfly nymphs, the water beetle *Dytiscus marginalis* should not be given to smaller salamander and newt species.

A commonly seen food item in the pet stores is the mealworm. While some larger salamander species are happy to accept them, they should never be given without supplements. Nutritionally speaking, mealworms are an incomplete diet.

insects sent from the breeders. Some producers are glad to supply insects regularly by mail order. Let us briefly discuss the more usual types of cultured livefood.

Mealworms

Not really worms, but the larvae of the flour beetle *Tenebrio molitor*, they are readily accepted by most salamanders. Mealworms can be obtained in any quantity from dealers or breeders. Once you have your initial stock, they are relatively easy to cultivate. Allow a few of the mealworms to pupate and metamorphose into adult beetles (these are brown and about 8 mm (⅜ in) long). The adult beetles are placed in a container with a close-fitting but ventilated (gauze) lid, along with a 5 cm (2 in)-layer of food mixture (bran and crushed oats is ideal). Place a piece of burlap over the food

mixture and put a couple of pieces of carrot or a similar vegetable on top to provide moisture. The beetles will soon mate and lay eggs in the food mixture. It takes about 7 days for the eggs to hatch into tiny mealworms, and these develop to full size in about 15 weeks. By starting a new culture each month, a regular supply of mealworms of all sizes will be available. For the best results, cultures should be kept at temperatures of 25 to 30°C (77 to 86°F).

Crickets

A very popular livefood for many insectivorous pets in recent years has been cultured crickets. They are relatively easy to breed and handle and are a very nutritious food item for your salamanders. Several species of cricket may be available, but the most commonly encountered are domestic or field species of the genera *Acheta* and *Gryllus*. There are now specialist "cricket farms" which breed crickets on a commercial basis and from which you can obtain your cultures. Crickets are useful in that they come in various sizes from ⅛ in to 1 in depending on what stage of the life cycle they are in, so you will have a size of cricket to suit most sizes of salamander! Crickets may be propagated in a ventilated box, with the

females to deposit their eggs in. With optimum conditions, the eggs will hatch in about 3 weeks, and the young can be reared to various sizes.

Cockroaches

These unpopular insects are abundant in all areas, even in inner cities, and are usually not too difficult to find in quantity. Like crickets, they are a nutritious livefood for amphibians, and several

If you can acquire them, small grasshoppers make a good meal. This particular specimen is the African Locust, *Schistocera migratoria*, often bred in captivity as a live food.

temperature maintained at about 26°C (79°F). They may be fed on a mixture of bran and crushed oats, plus a little green food or raw root vegetable. A piece of water-soaked cotton wool in a dish will provide additional moisture and will be used by gravid

species may be cultured if given similar conditions to the crickets described above. The tiny, first-instar nymphs make excellent food for smaller salamanders and newly metamorphosed newts. When breeding insects, especially cockroaches,

One of the easiest food items for a keeper to acquire is the cricket. Crickets are sold in virtually every pet store that sells herptiles and are highly recom-mended.

flies has thus been taken to a fine art. There is even a flightless (vestigal winged) variety that is useful for feeding to small salamanders as you dispense with the problem of having the flies escaping too easily. Fruitfly cultures and instructions on how to propagate them may be obtained from biological suppliers, some pet shops, and even by mail order. Large numbers of wild fruitflies may be collected if you place a heap of banana skins or some rotten fruit in a remote corner of the garden. During the warmer months, this will soon be teeming with fruitflies that can be simply collected with a fine-mesh net. Take care, however, not to upset any local fruit growers!

make sure they are kept in secure containers for obvious reasons.

Grasshoppers and Locusts

Often larger than crickets but still good food value, grasshoppers and locusts are somewhat more difficult to breed. Migratory locusts (*Schistocerca migratoria*) are bred commercially as livefood and it is perhaps wise just to buy a few occasionally as a treat for your larger pets.

Flies

Many of the thousands of fly species are ideal food for salamanders and newts. The relatively short life cycle of fruitflies makes them ideal for genetics research. The propagation of these little (⅛ in long)

Some of the common houseflies like *Musca* and *Fannia* species are also suitable for small to medium sized salamanders, while the larger greenbottles (*Lucilia* species, for example) and bluebottles (*Calliphora* species, for example) are suitable for your larger pets. Adequate supplies of flies may be collected in a flytrap during the the warmer parts of the year. A fairly convenient method of acquiring flies is to purchase maggots from a bait shop, if there is one in your area. The maggots themselves make a reasonable food for larger salamanders, but do not use them in quantity as they have a very tough skin and can be difficult for your pets to digest; just one or two occasionally are adequate. It is best to keep the maggots in containers of clean bran or sawdust and allow them to pupate. In a few days the adult flies (which are more easily digestible than the maggots) will emerge. Place a few pupae in a small plastic lunch box with a fly-

Earthworms

Earthworms and brandlings may be purchased from bait suppliers or can be collected in the garden or elsewhere; "worm farms" are now fairly common and some can be obtained through mail order. Worms are an excellent, highly nutritious food for salamanders. Large worms can be chopped into pieces for smaller animals and, as pieces of earthworm continue to wriggle for some time after being chopped, they are usually accepted readily by many species. A regular supply of

Every now and then, a keeper of aquatic species such as this Alpine Newt, *Triturus alpestris*, will get lucky and obtain a specimen that eats pelleted fish food.

sized hole in the lid and the flies will escape singly. Some salamanders will soon learn the location of this food source and will patiently wait near the box for flies to emerge.

earthworms can be collected by placing a pile of wet, dead leaves in a shady corner and covering it with a piece of sacking. By spraying the sacking with water regularly, earthworms will soon be attracted to the area and will congregate among the decaying leaves. They may then be collected at say, weekly intervals. As one supply becomes exhausted, you can start again in another spot. Clean potting mixture is an ideal medium in which to store earthworms for a week or so.

Whiteworms

These tiny worms (*Enchytraeus* species) can be purchased as cultures complete with instructions for further propagation. They are a useful food supply for newly metamorphosed newts and for very small salamander species.

Tubifex

These are slender, reddish colored aquatic worms which can often be obtained from aquatics suppliers. They are a nutritious food and are especially suitable for small aquatic salamanders, newts, and advanced larvae. As tubifex worms are often collected at sewage outlets or from similar locations, it is advisable to wash them under a slowly running tap for several hours before feeding them to your animals.

Vitamin/Mineral Supplements

Salamanders that generally are provided with a wide selection of livefoods are unlikely to suffer nutritional disturbances arising from mineral or vitamin deficiencies. Should a variety of live invertebrates be in short supply, however (during the winter, for example, when we have to make do with cultured foods such as mealworms or crickets over relatively long periods), it is advisable to give a regular multivitamin/mineral supplement, say two or three times per week. Suitable vitamin/mineral preparations may be obtained in fluid, powder, or tablet form from drug stores, pet shops, and veterinarians. Powders are probably the most suitable, as they can be dusted directly onto the livefood. The insects may be placed in a small container and the powder dusted over them. A gentle shake will ensure each insect has a film of powder over its surface; the insects are then given to your pets in the normal manner.

Non-live Foods

Many aquatic salamanders will take strips of meat or fish; some will even take trout pellets or other manufactured foods.

Do not provide fatty meat or fish as it will pollute the water more readily than lean meat, which is altogether a more healthy proposition. Lean, raw, beef-heart cut into fine strips is one of the best meats to use. Never provide your aquatic salamanders with more than the amphibians can eat in a few minutes, otherwise the water will soon be fouled.

Feeding Strategies

It is not necessary to feed salamanders every day; to do so may lead to obesity or lethargy. A good strategy is to feed three times per week, say Monday, Wednesday, and Friday.

Feed only as much as will be taken in a few minutes. You will need to experiment for a time before you ascertain the ideal quantities to give. Terrestrial species are usually attracted to their prey by movement, so in most cases it is pointless to give dead food. However, some of the larger terrestrial salamanders may be trained to take small pieces of meat by placing it in front of them and jiggling it with a very fine broom straw. Uneaten food, especially pieces of meat, fish, etc., should always be removed from the terrarium as soon as possible.

The Long-toed Salamander, *Ambystoma macro-dactylum*, may recognize prey only if it is moving about. Thus, you could conceivably offer it a piece of raw meat by jiggling the meat from forceps or the end of a broomstraw.

Hygiene and General Care

The general care of your salamanders and newts is closely linked with hygiene. or art of preserving good health and preventing disease. Cleanliness is, of

If you are keeping your caudates in a soil-based tank, it is a wise idea to replace the bedding every week or so. You can purchase fresh potting soil in bags or simply take some from the outdoors. Beware, however, of the inclusion of fertilizers, plant foods, etc., in some of the commercial varieties.

Animals confined to a relatively small space, such as in the terrarium, are completely reliant on their keeper for their welfare and general health, and this includes the application of good hygienic practices. When hearing the word hygiene, many people immediately conjure up thoughts of soaps and disinfectants. Here we are using the word in its most general sense: the science

course, a very important aspect of hygiene, but so is providing your terrarium inmates with optimum conditions for a stress-free, contented life. In itself stress can be a factor which reduces an animal's normal resistance to disease, so we must ensure that our animals's accommodations are as near to natural as possible.

In general, amphibians are not capable of easily

adapting to conditions that are alien to them. Just imagine how a salamander must feel after it is removed from a cool, damp, dark, leafy forest and placed in a glass box containing hard, chlorinated tap-water, then kept at room temperature day and night with the lights left on until midnight. Common sense will tell you that this is just the thing to cause stress and almost certain illness.

amphibian's health. Having a very sensitive and absorbent skin, amphibians can absorb lethal amounts of chemicals before you even realize what is happening. Use pond or river water whenever possible. If you can collect rainwater, this is ideal, especially that which has been standing for several days in a water tank. If you have no alternative but to use

Every captive salamander and newt should be checked regularly for signs of ill health. Do your own specimens look as healthy and well-developed as this *Pseudo-eurycea belli*?

As we have already discussed, photoperiod, light intensity, and temperature should be made similar to that found in the amphibian's native habitat. Excessive chlorine, copper, hardness, and/or acidity in various domestic water supplies can be dangerous to an

tapwater, allow it to stand for at least 24 hours to allow free chlorine to disperse before it is used.

ACQUISITION OF SPECIMENS

One important aspect of hygiene is to ensure that your new animals are free of disease, especially if you are going to introduce them to your existing, disease-free stock. Wild-captured salamanders and newts are almost always healthy, though they may carry some relatively harmless parasites. However, capture and confinement can induce stress, so try and make this as trauma-free as possible!

If you are going to purchase your amphibians from a pet shop, breeder, or dealer, first impressions of the premises can be important. The manner in which animals are commercially trapped, transported, and/or confined for wholesale and retail sale can be extremely stressful. Legislation in many countries now tries to ensure that captive animals, even "lowly" ones, get the best treatment possible. There will, however, always be a minority of animal dealers out to make a quick buck, so never purchase animals from premises that are dirty, untidy, and smelly, with overcrowded tanks. You will often see dead specimens mixed up with the live ones in such premises. A good animal dealer will be concerned about the welfare of every animal in his possession and will be proud to keep and display them in the cleanest and most hygienic of conditions.

Before purchase, all specimens should be individually examined to ensure they are in sound health; select only those that are plump and have sleek, unblemished skin. The eyes should be open and bright, with correctly shaped pupils. Avoid specimens with sunken abdomens and exaggeration of the bones; this is a sign of malnutrition, which may have been brought on by some other disease or by lack of proper care. Specimens with open wounds or injuries or with sores or tumors on the skin should be refused. Look for traces of fungus or bacterial infection. Avoid specimens with obvious eye disorders. Specimens should be wary of the hand and should attempt to crawl away when touched. Do not accept specimens which show no fight, fright, or flight.

HANDLING

Most salamanders dislike being handled, and a warm, sweaty hand is not only uncomfortable to them, the salt content of the sweat can be dangerous to them if you hold the delicate little creatures for too long. Salamanders should therefore not be regarded as pets to fondle, but to admire; they should thus be handled as little as possible and even then only for examination purposes. On being handled, many amphibians will release the fluid contents of the cloaca. This is a salamander's reserve supply of body fluid hands before handling and rinse them well in clear water, leaving them wet. A small specimen can be gently cupped in the hands and examined by spreading the fingers. Larger, robust specimens should be gripped gently but firmly round the body with their limbs restrained between

As disappointing as it may be, virtually no caudates like being handled. Some, like this Ensatina, *Ensatina eschscholtzi*, are particularly delicate.

and must be replaced, so ensure that a salamander that has voided its reserves has access to water as soon as possible. Amphibians do not normally drink in the true sense but are able to absorb moisture through the skin.

One time when it will be necessary to handle a salamander is when you are contemplating its purchase. Always wash the the fingers. Aquatic salamanders and larvae can be caught in a net made from soft material and examined without any need for handling, other than moving the net material away from the body of the animal.

Remember that many salamanders and newts have powerful protective poisons which they release from glands in the skin.

Some of these can be extremely irritating if you get them in your eyes or mucous membranes. Therefore, always wash your hands thoroughly after handling amphibians. Some species are also unable to tolerate the poisons of others, so don't keep more than one species together unless you are absolutely sure they are tolerant of each other.

TRANSPORT

Probably the most stressful time for captive amphibians is capture and subsequent transport. From time to time, further transport may involve movement from room to room, premises to premises, even from one country to another. The ideal situation is when the animals arrive at their destination in a state no worse than at the point of departure. Although it has been proven time and again that most animals suffer stress during transportation, it is important that we make this process as trauma-free as possible for them and thus keep stress to a minimum.

Plastic "lunch boxes" with a number of ventilation holes drilled in the lid are useful for transporting terrestrial salamanders. Such boxes are best loosely packed with damp sphagnum moss or water weed to keep the amphibians moist and to prevent them from being injured if the boxes are dropped or roughly handled. The animals should be taken as quickly as possible to their destination, via the shortest or fastest route. Transport boxes should never be left exposed to the

Although the Eastern Tiger Salamander, *Ambystoma tigrinum tigrinum*, is primarily found on land, when transporting one you should always have it in a container filled with a damp substrate like moist paper towels.

sun's rays or left in a parked car in sunny weather as overheating can occur quickly and dramatically. On the other hand, sub-tropical and tropical species will require protection from chilling during cold weather, and in such cases it is wise to pack the transport boxes in some kind of an insulated container (a styrofoam box, for example).

Aquatic salamanders and newts should be placed in water inside doubled (one inside the other), waterproof plastic bags. The bag is then inflated with air or oxygen and sealed with a knot or a rubber band. This is a tried and tested way of carrying aquarium fish, and a number of the bags can be transported in a styrofoam box. When transport containers are being sent over long distances or by public transport, it is wise to pack the styrofoam boxes within stronger wooden crates.

QUARANTINE

New animals destined to join your existing collection must first undergo a period of quarantine to ensure that they do not introduce any infectious ailment that could cause a disastrous epidemic among all of your

When keeping any amphibian, strict attention to cleanliness is absolutely crucial. Even an animal as hardy as this Jordan's Salamander, *Plethodon jordani*, can succumb to the evils of a filthy tank in a matter of days.

animals. It is best to always have a suitable quarantine tank available. A simple terrarium with the minimum of decorations but with the usual life support systems and hiding places is adequate. It is best kept in a separate room from the main stock. Your new stock should be placed in the quarantine terrarium and observed carefully over the next 21 days. It should be safe to introduce the new stock to your existing animals if they are still fit and healthy after the quarantine period.

HYGIENE IN GENERAL

The humid conditions required by salamanders in terraria unfortunately are also the exact conditions favored by fungi, bacteria, and other unpleasant organisms. Many of these organisms are not necessarily pathogenic in themselves but can produce noxious by-products as well as look unpleasant. Use only sterile materials when setting up, and get the right balance between ventilation and humidity by trial and error in order to reduce the danger of bacterial or fungal proliferation.

Always wash your hands after handling animals or furnishings in one tank, before moving on to the next one. Even if there is no obvious sign of disease, this will ensure that you are not the cause of an epidemic among your charges. Terraria should be routinely cleaned out at regular intervals. This should consist only of scrubbing the terrarium and its furnishings with clean water then rinsing with plenty more of the same. Allowing furnishings and accessories to dry out naturally in the warmth of the sun is an ideal safe way of disinfecting them before returning them to the terrarium. If a disease outbreak should occur, isolate the patient(s) in a hospital terrarium in a separate room. If you are unable to identify the disease, dead specimens should be sent for autopsy (ask your veterinarian for advice on this) or destroyed by burning. Empty the terrarium and destroy plants, logs, etc., by burning. Rocks, gravel, etc., can be discarded or sterilized by boiling. The terrarium should be scrubbed out with a 10% solution of household bleach or with a veterinary povidone-iodine preparation, then thoroughly swilled out with clean, hot water and left to stand for 24 hours before being thoroughly swilled again before use.

HIBERNATION

During the colder parts of the year, salamanders from cool-temperate, sub-tropical, and montane climates hibernate. They may bury themselves in mud at the bottom of ponds or descend into deep subterranean burrows where they are protected against freezing. A

Species that occur in warmer climates, such as this *Bolitoglossa altama-zonica*, do not have to be hibernated in the general sense, but simply given a period of "cooling" at a reduced temperature.

salamander's basic metabolism is reduced dramatically during hibernation. Being in a torpor, it requires very little oxygen and no food at all, though it will hopefully have stored adequate reserves during the preceding summer. While hibernating species can be kept "awake" all year long in captivity, it is likely that this will seriously interfere with their reproductive cycles. It is the period of hibernation and the slow warming, coupled with the extended photoperiod in the spring, that brings such amphibians into breeding condition.

In captivity, however, our salamanders will make do with a period of simulated hibernation without decreasing prospects of successful breeding. To get them into hibernating mode, gradually lower the temperature and shorten the photoperiod in the terrarium over a period of about 14 days. Stop feeding the animals and remove the terrarium to a frost-free shed or garage, where the temperature should be maintained at not less than 4°C (39°F) and not higher than 10°C (50°F) for about 8 to 10 weeks. An alternative method is to place the salamanders in slightly damp moss in a plastic container which is then placed in a fridge and kept at about 4 to 5°C (39 to 41°F) for a similar time. The reverse procedure (gradual increase of temperature and photoperiod over several days) should be carried out at the end of the period of simulated hibernation.

SOME COMMON DISEASES AND THEIR TREATMENT

Amphibians are remarkably resistant to diseases and most cases of ill health among captive stock can usually be blamed on some inadequacy in the care. Recent research has made good inroads into the diagnosis and treatment of amphibian diseases though some cures are unfortunately still "hit and miss" affairs. There are a few veterinarians who devote themselves to the study of the more unusual types of pets, including amphibians, and your local veterinarian should be able to communicate with one or more of these experts if he is unsure himself. Some of the more common afflictions follow.

Nutritional Deficiencies

Usually occur as a result of a lack of certain minerals or vitamins in the diet and are likely to occur in

salamanders fed on a monotonous diet of say, mealworms. It is essential your animals have access to a large variety of foodstuffs. As an additional safeguard against nutritional disturbances, give a routine application of a powdered multivitamin/mineral supplement.

Open Wounds

Open wounds or injuries to the skin may be caused when salamanders attempt to escape from terraria, etc. This usually occurs among newly captured specimens, which should be left undisturbed until they become accustomed to their new surroundings, after which time such injuries will be less likely. Wounds are subject to bacterial infections which

are potentially lethal, so treatment with an antibiotic may be necessary. Obtain advice from your veterinarian before applying any antiseptic preparations (some antiseptics which are quite safe for humans are lethal to amphibians).

Bacterial Infections

One or more of several obscure kinds of bacterial infection (including *Alcaligenes*, *Mimea*, *Pseudomonas*, and *Vibrio*) may occasionally be contracted by captive salamanders. Symptoms are varied and may include listlessness, accumulations of mucus on the skin, skin blemishing, loss of weight and condition, refusal to feed, and deterioration of the extremities (tip of tail

If you have a salamander that does not look as healthy as this Flatwoods Salamander, *Ambystoma cingulatum*, then it would not be advisable to hibernate it. Chances are it will not be able to withstand the physical strain.

Aquatic newts are generally hardy, but small bodies of water can become disease-infested very quickly. Therefore, a keeper must change the animals's quarters often. Shown is the California Newt, *Taricha torosa.*

and digits). Such diseases may respond to treatment by one of a number of antibiotics.

Aeromonas Infection

Another bacterial disease, and one that is probably the most dangerous disease of captive amphibians. Caused by the organism *Aeromonas hydrophila,* symptoms include the reddening of the skin, especially on the belly and the underside of the limbs. Infected animals become disinterested and lethargic and they should be immediately isolated. If caught in its early stages, *Aeromonas* may be treated by immersing the infected animal for about 15 seconds in a 2% solution of copper sulfate or potassium permanganate. The use of an antibiotic such as tetracycline may also help. Consult a veterinarian for advice about this lethal disease.

Salmonella

This is known to cause anemia in axolotls and probably in other aquatic

salamanders as well. In an infected axolotl, the internal organs become inflamed, the animal loses condition, and will die if untreated. The animal is immersed in a solution of 1 gm terramycin to 100 L of water and this solution is changed daily for 5 days. Then place the animal in a 1% solution of common salt for a week before repeating the terramycin treatment.

Caution: Terrestrial species will not survive treatment by immersion.

Fungal Infections

Saprolegnia and other fungal infections can be troublesome in aquatic amphibians and in larvae. The disease is seen as areas of inflamed skin surrounded by whitish tissue. Untreated, these infections can prove fatal. If caught in its early stages a fungus infection can be treated by immersing the animal in a 2% solution of malachite green or Mercurochrome for 5 minutes, repeating after 24 hours if symptoms do not improve. Larvae should be treated by keeping them in a solution of 0.001% chloramine (paratoluol sodium sulfonchloramide) for 24 hours, then in fresh water for 3 days, and repeat the initial treatment.

Reproduction and Captive Breeding

Reproductive behavior in salamander species is fairly diverse. While any atypical salamander in the genus *Ambystoma* known as the Axolotl.

Two Spanish Ribbed Newts, *Pleurodeles waltl*, in a breeding clasp. Interestingly, the male is on the bottom.

special reproductive habits of species included in this book will be briefly described in the species chapter, a more detailed look at a couple of typical life cycles of aquatic species, followed by a brief general summary on the captive breeding of salamanders and newts, will not go amiss. As examples we will take a typical newt in the genus *Triturus* and a somewhat

LIFE HISTORY OF THE MARBLED NEWT

The Marbled Newt (*Triturus marmoratus*) is one of the larger and more beautiful "typical" newts of Europe and has two subspecies. The start of the breeding season varies with the part of the range, and the newts usually make for the breeding ponds from late February to early April. It is a combination of increases in photoperiod

Most of the brook salamanders, genus *Eurycea*, are fairly difficult to breed but not impossible. This poses a true challenge to the interested hobbyist. Shown is a pair of Three-lined Salamanders, *Eurycea longicauda guttolineata.*

and temperature which triggers the breeding response. Although not overly fussy in its selection of breeding ponds, it usually prefers small to medium, but fairly deep, densely vegetated ponds with clear water. What criteria influence the newts's choice of pond are not known, but while one body of water may be used prolifically, another apparently similar pond in the vicinity may be totally ignored (though other newt species may breed there).

Adult Marbled Newts reach up to 15 cm (6 in) in length. The skin is granular and the male has a relatively smooth-edged, high dorsal crest with a deep indentation at the end of the body and start of the tail. The crest diminishes considerably outside the breeding season but usually remains evident. In place of the crest, the female has a shallow vertebral groove running the length of the body. The Marbled Newt can probably be regarded as the most attractive of the genus (with the possible exception of *T. vittatus*). The color is basically a vivid green with a conspicuous black marbling, this being bolder on the male than on the female. The underside is grayish to brownish, often marked with black and white. The females and juveniles possess a narrow, reddish vertebral stripe. In nuptial dress, the male develops his high crest, which is banded with alternate black and dull white vertical bars. His general color becomes more intense and he develops a silvery stripe along each side of the tail.

The amorous male attempts to attract a suitable female by performing a courtship dance, usually at a water depth of 30 to 45 cm (12 to 18 in) on the pond floor. The courtship "arena" is usually an area devoid of vegetation. Approaching a prospective mate, he will nudge her, and if she is not interested in his advances she will simply swim away. If she is receptive, however, she will then stay her ground and await further developments. Initially, the male rubs noses with the female

several times. Then he bends his body into a rigid bow while pointing the tip of his tail in the direction of his bride. He next plants his forelimbs firmly on the substrate or other solid surface to give him stability as he wriggles the rear part of his body and tail vigorously. He simultaneously releases an "aphrodisiac" scent from his cloaca, and this is carried in the direction of the female in water currents he creates by his actions.

This nuptial dance can continue for 20 minutes or more, and the female often apears to be hypnotized by his performance. At length, the male deposits a spermatophore on the substrate near the female and then seems to lose all further interest in the proceedings. However, by now the female is usually sufficiently aroused to absorb the

Note the feathery gills on this larval Long-toed Salamander, *Ambystoma macro-dactylum*. These will vanish before the animal becomes terrestrial.

The feathery filaments on the gill stalks of larval salamanders allow the animals to breathe. The reason they are reddish in color is because they are filled with blood.

spermatophore into her cloaca, ready to fertilize her eggs which are already developing.

Over the following week or so, the female deposits an average of 200 to 300 eggs singly, usually on the underside of the leaf of a water plant. The eggs have a sticky, jelly-like coating that adheres quite firmly to the leaf, which the female may bend around the egg for added protection. The tiny larvae hatch in a few days. At first they are completely limbless and about 8 mm (⅜ in) in length. They possess three feathery external gills on each side of the neck just behind the head. The larvae will not feed as they will still be absorbing the contents of the yolk sac attached to the abdomen, but as soon as this is

accomplished, they will begin to hunt for tiny aquatic organisms, on which they will feed voraciously. The larvae will grow and gradually develop into recognizable little newts about 5 cm (2 in) long by the end of the summer and, like the adults, will leave the water to seek their fortunes on dry land.

The adults often remain in the water until well into the summer. For the remainder of the summer and the first part of the fall, newts of all ages hunt insects in the undergrowth, fattening themselves up for the period of hibernation which is to follow. During this time, the newts are largely crepuscular and nocturnal, hiding during the day under logs, ground debris, and in root systems, often in the burrows of other animals. The adults lose their breeding dress before leaving the water, the male loses his crest, and colors become somewhat duller.

T. marmoratus spends much of the winter in hibernation in most parts of its range, though it may become active in mild, wet conditions. As the hours of daylight decrease and the

temperatures diminish, both juvenile and adult newts seek out suitable spots in which to take their winter rest. They may burrow deep down in loose earth or use the burrows of

the newts into renewed activity and they congregate at their breeding ponds. The young of the previous season should not breed until their third year.

other animals until they reach a depth out of reach of the heaviest winter frosts. (Species which normally hibernate in the wild can be kept in captivity without hibernation simply by providing extra warmth and light in the winter. However, this confuses their natural rhythms and the animals are not only unlikely to breed, but the length of their lives is likely to be correspondingly reduced. It is therefore advisable to allow your animals to experience at least a token period of hibernation at reduced temperatures.) The cycle starts over again when the warmth and light of the springtime sun stimulates

LIFE CYCLE OF THE AXOLOTL

The Axolotl, *Ambystoma mexicanum*, is perhaps the most widely kept of all amphibians and is an extremely popular pet in many countries. This is because over the years the Axolotl has been almost domesticated. It is also a popular species for biological research and education. Interestingly, in Australia (where it is commonly referred to as the "Mexican Walking Fish") it is, in fact, the only caudate legally allowed to be kept as a pet outside zoos or research establishments.

The first Europeans to see live Axolotls were probably the Spanish conquistadores who arrived in Mexico in the 16th

Unlike most other herptiles, many salamanders breed during the colder times of the year. These Ensatinas, *Ensatina eschscholtzi*, for example, will start their reproductive cycle during mid-autumn and continue throughout the winter.

century. The Axolotl was said to be partially sacred to the original natives of the Lakes Xochimilcho and Chalco areas (near the present Mexico City), but it still appeared on the menu at certain times of the year. Wild Axolotls may still be found in those same lakes today, but they now have protected status.

Despite its relative familiarity, the Axolotl is a fascinating creature deserving a place in the collection of every salamander keeper at least in some period of his or her hobby. It is especially valuable to the beginner, being relatively easy to keep, feed, and breed. Another great advantage of Axolotl keeping is that all available specimens have been bred in captivity, so there is no depletion of wild populations.

When sexually mature, Axolotls may reach a length of 25 cm (10 in), though the average is only about 17 to 20 cm (7 to 8 in). The "normal"- colored Axolotl, like its wild counterpart, is dark sooty brown with even darker brown to black spots and blotches. The underside is somewhat lighter. Captive stocks have produced a number of color mutations, including albinos, goldens, olives, and pieds, the latter

probably being the most unusual. The Axolotl has a broad, shovel-like snout and a flattened head with a wide mouth. Its small, lidless eyes are wide-spaced but oriented toward the top of the head. It has short, robust limbs spaced well-apart on the sturdy body. A number of vertical (costal) grooves are apparent along the flanks. There are four fingers and five toes respectively on the fore- and hind-limbs. A smooth-edged, semi-transparent crest starts just behind the head and runs along the vertebral column into the laterally flattened tail where it becomes wider. The crest also continues along the underside of the tail, which is used by the animal to swim and steer. The limbs are mostly used for walking about on the substrate, but may also assist in braking and steering when the animal is swimming. A very prominent Axolotl feature is its pair of three-lobed feathery gills which project up to 2 cm (¾ in) on either side of the head. These are deep reddish brown in normal specimens but bright crimson in white or golden specimens.

In the wild, Axolotls generally do not metamorphose into terrestrial forms, but they

can be persuaded to change into typical adult salamanders in captivity. Normal-colored specimens will become dark gray with yellow spots; the tail will become round in section and the skin will become smoother. Metamorphosis may be encouraged by gradually reducing the water depth over a period of several months. Once the water is about 2 cm (¾ in) deep, the animals will be forced to start taking atmospheric oxygen. The process can also be halted at any stage almost up to full metamorphosis by again increasing the water

process is irreversible and the creature would drown if forcibly kept below water.

The process of metamorphosis is evidently influenced by the amount of thyroxine in the thyroid gland. If injected with a small quantity or immersed in a solution of this hormone, Axolotls will develop into their terrestrial form. The introduction of minute quantities of iodine into the water in which Axolotls are kept has been found to promote the production of thyroxine by the salamanders, also resulting in complete metamorphosis. The

The Axolotl, *Ambystoma mexicanum*, has been bred repeatedly in captivity. Larvae can be fed on tiny tubifex and bloodworms like those shown here.

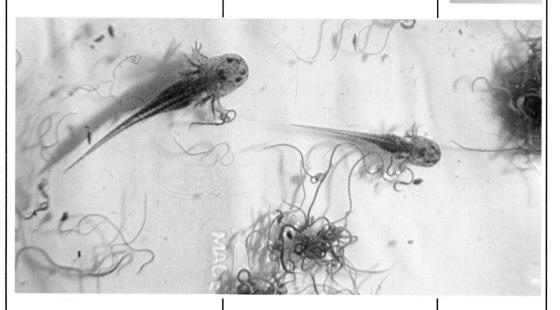

depth and allowing the partially absorbed gills to redevelop. However, once the gills have been completely absorbed, the

process of remaining as a larva and being able to reproduce in that state is known as neoteny, while such reproduction itself is known as paedogenesis.

An interesting capability of the Axolotl (shared with many other salamanders, especially larvae), is its ability to regenerate limbs or gill filaments which have been lost accidentally or to predators (the latter often being other, larger Axolotls). A new

Two California Slender Salamanders, *Batrachoseps attenuatus*.

appendage, usually perfect in every detail, will grow within a few weeks to replace the missing one!

Axolotls may be housed in simple aquaria, no more than four specimens to a tank, about 60 x 30 cm (2 ft x 1 ft). Water depth should be somewhere between 20 and 30 cm (8 to 12 in). Axolotls prefer water that is neutral to slightly alkaline (pH 7.0 to 7.6). Clean aquarium gravel and a few pebbles for decoration may be placed on the substrate. The tank should be equipped with an aerator and a filter.

Supplementary heating is unnecessary since Axolotls will fare well at room temperatures and can tolerate a range of temperatures, though they seem to thrive best at 17 to 20°C (63 to 68°F).

Axolotls have voracious appetites and wild specimens will eat almost any prey they are capable of overpowering. Captive specimens may be fed on lean raw meat, which they seem to find by a combination of smell and touch. This, however, does not constitute a balanced diet and should only be a supplement of various livefoods such as earthworms, slugs, snails, mealworms, crickets, etc. Do not overfeed and allow uneaten food to remain in the tank as you will be asking for trouble (fouling, smells, pollution, and ultimate death of your Axolotls). Should livefood be in short supply at any time, you should add a multivitamin/mineral powder to the lean meat by scouring the meat into the powder.

Wild Axolotls breed toward the end of the

winter months (usually February), when melting snows from surrounding mountains temporarily reduce temperatures in the lakes. Breeding may also take place when the water cools in autumn. Compromise conditions can be provided by adding ice cubes to the captive Axolotl tank, thus submitting the amphibians to thermal shock. Animals kept normally at 20°C (68°F) may have their water temperature temporarily reduced to 10 to 12°C (50 to 54°F). This may be done at any time of the year, but best successes take place from December to mid-July. Adult Axolotls of both sexes are similar in size and shape, though the male may have a slightly broader head and the female a plumper body. When sexually mature, the

male will also have a markedly swollen cloacal region. Axolotls may breed from the age of 9 to 12 months onward, but best results occur when the animals are 30 months old. As the animals age, they become less productive. Most captive Axolotls will live 6 to 10 years if given optimum conditions, and I recently have been informed about a specimen that lived in a tank for 16 years.

The male courts the female by making stylized movements with his body. These will include bending the body almost double and rapidly wriggling the tail. Eventually he will deposit a spermatophore on the substrate close to the female before temporarily losing interest in the proceedings. However, the male is capable of repeating

In this adult pair of California Tiger Salamanders, *Ambystoma tigrinum californiense*, you can clearly see the differences between the male (bottom) and the female (top). The male is more slender and the female is more plump. Also, the head is slightly more stout on the female.

the procedure several times and may deposit as many as 15 spermatophores. The receptive female will take the spermatophore into her cloaca where the stored spermatozoa from the spermatophore will fertilize the eggs as they are being laid. Oviposition begins about 48 hours after fertilization and up to 800 eggs are laid in batches of 10 to 30 on the leaves of water plants or on substrate debris.

It is advisable to keep the sexes separate until a breeding response is required. Then a single pair is housed together in a small tank. A temperature reduction from the normal 17 to 20°C (63 to 68°F), down to 10 to 12°C (50 to 54°F) will usually result in almost immediate mating behavior, and egglaying can be expected within 48 hours. It is best to provide a number of pieces of plastic pipe (12 mm— ½ in electrical conduit is ideal) jammed across the width of the container at about half the water's depth, ensuring you leave plenty of room for the animals to swim between them. Most of the eggs will then be laid on these tubes. After laying, the adults can be removed back to their respective stock tanks. The water temperature in the

breeding tank can then be slowly raised back to 17 to 20°C (63 to 68°F). The water should be fresh, well-aerated, and free of chlorine, and the eggs should hatch within 14 days. Eggs that turn milky white are infertile and should be removed with a pipette before they decay and pollute the water. Upon hatching, the tiny Axolotls will remain close to the egg case and they will not require food for the first 48 hours as they will still be feeding from the egg sac, but after this they may be given infusoria, brine shrimp, and/or water fleas. Pounded lean meat and hard-boiled egg yolk may also be given, but in extremely small quantities to avoid pollution of the water. The larvae soon become active and at 5 days of age they should be separated into batches and placed in aerated containers of water about 20 cm (8 in) deep. Well-fed youngsters will grow rapidly and you will soon be able to give them larger food items such as tubifex, whiteworms, mosquito larvae, and small earthworms. Properly cared for and given a varied diet, young Axolotls can reach sexual maturity in as little as 6 months, but for best results it is advisable to wait until they are 9 to 12 months old before this is attempted.

Pleurodeles waltl (the Spanish Ribbed Newt) can be induced to spawn by

Salamander eggs are extremely delicate and should not be disturbed under any circumstances. Note the egg strands lying around this female Axolotl, *Ambystoma mexicanum.*

GENERAL

The majority of salamander and newt species require external stimuli to promote a courtship and mating response. Species from cool temperate regions, for example, usually breed in the spring, shortly after hibernation, and are influenced by increases in temperature, photoperiod, and light intensity. Tropical species may be influenced by changes in humidity, either seasonal or coincidental.

Some species can be persuaded to breed in captivity by injecting them with certain hormones.

injecting 250 International Units of H.C.G. (human chorionic gonadotrophin), a hormone which is produced by pregnant women. In fact, frogs of the genus *Xenopus* were once used in pregnancy tests for women before more convenient methods were discovered, and there is no reason to doubt that certain salamander species could have been used in the same way. Needless to say, if you contemplate using hormone injections to encourage your salamanders to breed, this should be done with the help of a veterinarian or licensed animal technician.

Although many wild salamanders and newts have regular breeding cycles, the Spanish Ribbed Newt, *Pleurodeles waltl*, seems to mate at any time of the year, conditions permitting.

Most seasonal breeders that breed in larger bodies of water can be given similar treatment to the Axolotl, though the water temperature, of course, will depend on the native habitat of the species in question. For cool temperate and sub-tropical species, pairs are introduced in the spring, after beginning to gradually increase temperature and photoperiod. These increases should continue until a maximum of 20°C (68°F) and a 15-hour period

done by rearing them in an aqua-terrarium with a sloping "bank." Alternatively, they may be reared in shallow water in which large flat stones are placed so that they just break the water's surface.

Where large numbers of offspring are produced, you will probably need to cull off some of the larvae in order to prevent overcrowding, and it is much better to rear a small number of fit, healthy specimens rather than end up with numerous

of "daylight" has been reached. Amphibious species which live on land after metamorphosis should be given facilities to leave the water as soon as they are ready. This can be

weaklings. As the larvae grow, weed out the smaller and deformed specimens and dispose of them. Do not release exotic specimens which could be a future ecological hazard.

Choice of Species

Many factors will influence the choice of species you will keep. Availability will, of course, be a major consideration, but personal taste may also play a role. Beginners are advised to start with inexpensive, "easier" species, before becoming more adventurous. As there are about 360 known caudate species, it will be impossible to discuss all of them in a volume of this size. However, most families and many of the better known genera will be mentioned, and a number of representative species will be selected for more detailed attention. Further hints on the care of species not covered in detail in this book may be gleaned from a good field guide, where notes on habits, habitat, and geographical range will give valuable clues on a strategy for captive husbandry.

In the following text, the descriptions of superfamilies have been largely ignored and the families are listed in the assumed evolutionary order. Family descriptions have been kept brief but the descriptions of sample genera will indicate the general familial characteristics. For the sake of convenience, genera and species have been placed in alphabetical order within the families. Subfamilies have been introduced where considered appropriate. Lengths given are the maximum to which an

The Ozark Hellbender, *Cryptobranchus alleganiensis bishopi*, needs a fully aquatic tank and a few hiding places. Most of the latter are constructed by securely piling rocks on each other.

adult specimen of that species may be expected to grow, though average adult sizes would be somewhat less.

FAMILY CRYPTOBRANCHIDAE

With two genera and only three species, this family includes the world's two largest salamanders in the genus *Andrias*. These are the Chinese Giant Salamander, *A. davidianus*, and the Japanese Giant Salamander, *A. japonicus*, which reach a maximum size of 1.8 and 1.4 m (6 ft and 4ft 8 in) respectively. As endangered species these giant salamanders are strictly protected and as such are unlikely to be legally available to the average enthusiast. The genus *Cryptobranchus* contains a single species.

Cryptobranchus alleganiensis (Hellbender)—

Length: 75 cm (30 in). Found in the central and eastern United States, the hellbender prefers fast-flowing rivers and streams, especially those with rocky bottoms, where it hides under rocks or in cavities during the day, coming out at night to hunt for food. This American relative of the Asian giant salamanders (*Andrias*) is a large, totally aquatic amphibian with a flattened head and body; a loose flap of skin runs along the lower flanks. It has relatively large limbs with four fingers and five toes.

There is a single pair of gill openings just behind the head, but no feathery gill filaments as seen in many other aquatic species. The color is grayish brown with darker mottling above, while the underside is lighter and uniform. The female is somewhat larger than the male. Hellbenders feed on a variety of invertebrates and vertebrates, and in captivity they will take strips of raw meat or fish. They should be kept only in very large, well-aerated aquaria with a stony substrate and caves for seclusion.

Supplementary heating is unnecessary, and there should be a reduced winter temperature. The animals breed in the late summer to fall, the male excavating a nest cavity beneath large flat rocks or submerged logs. The female lays 200 to 500 eggs in long strings which are sprayed with milt by the male then pushed together into a tangled mass in the nest cavity. The male guards the nest until the approximately 2.5 cm (1 in) larvae hatch in 2 to 3 months.

FAMILY SALAMANDRIDAE

Commonly called the family of typical salamanders and newts, there are 14 genera and some 53 species occuring in Eurasia and N. Africa. Only two genera, *Notophthalmus* and *Taricha*, occur in the New World.

Cynops pyrrhogaster (Red-bellied Newt)—Length 10 cm (4 in). One of seven species in its genus and a very popular terrarium

subject, this newt is dark chocolate brown above and brilliant, fiery red below. In the breeding season the male's tail becomes bluish or purplish. Found only on the Japanese islands of Honshu, Shikoku, and Kyushu, it is an almost totally aquatic newt (newly metamorphosed juveniles spend a few months on land before returning to water) that lives in well-vegetated ponds.

A closely related species (*C. ensicauda*) occurs on the Ryukyu Islands south of Japan. In captivity they require an aquarium with well-planted, aerated, and filtered water to a depth of 25 cm (10 in) and land areas, such as mossy rocks or tree roots, breaking the surface. Summer

The Hong Kong Newt, *Paramesotriton hongkongensis*, like most Asian newts, should be kept in cool water.

temperature should be maintained around 24°C (75°F) but can be reduced to 3 to 8°C (37 to 46°F) for a couple of months of simulated hibernation. They feed on small aquatic invertebrates. Breeding occurs early in the year when courtship and mating take place in water. The eggs are laid individually on the leaves of aquatic plants.

Notophthalmus viridescens viridescens (Red-spotted Newt)—Length 12 cm (5 in). This newt is very well known in the USA and is noted for the remarkable differences in appearance between the aquatic adults and the juvenile terrestrial form. Adults are smooth-skinned and yellowish to olive-brown above with dark-bordered red spots along each side of the body, sometimes almost forming a line. The underside is yellowish and there are small, dark spots all

over the body. The terrestrial juveniles, known as red efts, were once thought to be an entirely separate species. These have a rough skin texture and are bright reddish brown to orange all over, with spots of lighter red along the flanks. They are found in eastern North America from southern Canada and the Great Lakes region to Florida and eastern Texas. Adults are mainly aquatic, living in shallow, vegetated waters. In captivity, they require a

large aqua-terrarium which will support both the terrestrial and aquatic stages. Temperature should preferably not exceed 22°C (72°F) in summer and should be reduced to around 5°C (41°F) in winter for hibernation. Courtship occurs in water and 200 to 400 eggs are laid singly, attached to aquatic vegetation. Gilled larvae hatch in 3 to 8 weeks and these metamorphose into the red efts, which spend one or more years on land before returning to the water as mature adults.

Paramesotriton hongkongensis (Hong Kong Newt)—Length 15 cm (6 in). A member of a genus containing five species native to northern Indo-China and China, the Hong Kong Newt is confined to the island of Hong Kong and the adjacent Chinese mainland, where it occurs in the vegetated pools of mountain streams. It is uniform dark brown to black above while the underside is marked with numerous orange-red blotches that may extend onto the flanks. It remains in water throughout the year, breeding from November to February. About 120 eggs are attached singly to submerged plants. The young have external gills which disappear at metamorphosis about 8 months after hatching. In captivity, this species

The Eastern Red-spotted Newt, *Not-ophthalmus viridescens*, is a very common hobby animal, most prominently in the United States.

requires a cool, planted aquarium with filtered water and facilities to get onto land (rock or log breaking water surface). Feed on a variety of aquatic invertebrates, small earthworms, and very thin strips of lean beef-heart or liver.

Pleurodeles waltl (Spanish Ribbed Newt)— Length 30 cm (12 in). This is the largest European salamander, though relatively few specimens actually reach the maximum length. It is a heavily built animal with a broad, flattened head; the females are relatively plumper than the males. The skin is granular and there is a row of yellow or orange warty tubercles along each flank. The sharp tips of the ribs may protrude through these tubercles. The upper side is olive to grayish yellow with dark brown patches; they often become darker with age. Beneath, it is yellow to off white or gray, usually with darker blotches. It inhabits the southwestern two-thirds of the Iberian peninsula and Morocco, and occurs in watercourses, lakes, ponds, and irrigation systems. If water sources actually dry up, it will estivate in the mud until conditions again become favorable.

In captivity, it requires a planted aquarium with facilities to get onto land (a floating platform or a rock breaking the water surface). They will feed on larger invertebrates such as earthworms, freshwater shrimps, crickets, and so

A female Spanish Ribbed Newt, *Pleurodeles waltl*, can lay anywhere from 200 to 1000 eggs at a time.

The Rough-skinned Newt, *Taricha granulosa*, has been called the most aquatic newt in western North America.

on. They may also take small strips of lean meat. Maintain at 25°C (77°F) (summer) and reduce to around 8°C (46°F) for winter rest. Courtship occurs in the water, and the male deposits a spermatophore which is taken up by the female. Up to 1000 eggs are laid in clumps on water plants, roots, or submerged debris.

Taricha granulosa (Rough-skinned Newt)— Length 20 cm (8 in). The genus *Taricha* replaces *Notophthalmus* on the western coast of North America. The Rough-skinned Newt and its close relatives *T. rivularis* (Red-bellied newt) and *T. torosa* (California Newt) are very similar in general appearance. The Rough-skinned Newt, as its name implies, has a warty skin. It is light brown to black above with a sharply contrasting orange to yellow underside. When breeding, the male's skin becomes temporarily smooth and his tail becomes compressed. When alarmed or attacked by predators, this newt arches its body to expose the colorful underside in an effort to promote the fact that it has poisonous skin secretions. It ranges from northern California north to southeastern Alaska. It is mainly aquatic, keeping to permanent water. It may occasionally leave the water after heavy rains and search for terrestrial food items. Captive specimens should be provided with a large, planted aquarium with a small land area. Keep at 20°C (68°F) during summer and reduce to around 10°C (50°F) and cease to feed for a couple of months in winter. Feed on a variety of small aquatic invertebrates, crickets, and earthworms. It breeds from December to July, and the eggs are laid on aquatic

One of the first "popular" salamanders was the Fire Salamander, *Salamandra salamandra*, which does very well in captivity and is still widely available.

plants. In favorable conditions the larvae may metamorphose during the first season, but in colder areas this may take up to 2 years.

Salamandra salamandra (Fire Salamander)—Length 25 cm (10 in). This is the "original" salamander and subject of much folklore. The colorful European Fire Salamander is glossy black with bright yellow to orange markings arranged in spots, blotches, or stripes, depending on geographical variation. There are 11 subspecies occuring in western, central, and southern Europe, northwestern Africa, and parts of southwestern Asia, usually inhabiting heavily forested areas in hilly or mountainous country. It thrives in moist conditions, rarely far from water, and hides under ground litter during the day, emerging at night to forage for food. Captive specimens require a large, unheated aqua-terrarium with moving (aerated) water. Adequate refuges such as flat stones and hollow branches should be provided. These salamanders will feed on a variety of invertebrates including earthworms, slugs, and crickets, which they catch with their protrusible adhesive tongues. A period of hibernation in the winter at lowered temperatures is recommended. Courtship and mating occur on land and the female deposits developed larvae into suitable water.

Triturus alpestris (Alpine Newt)—Length 10 cm (4 in). This genus contains 12 species of typical European newts. The Alpine Newt is a small but attractive newt in which the female is larger and more robust than the slender male. In its terrestrial stage, the upper surface is dark brown to black while the belly is a uniform bright orange to carmine red. At breeding time, the male develops a low crest with alternating white and dark vertical bars. In both sexes the flanks become deep blue, marked with small dark spots. It ranges throughout central Europe from the western coast of France and the Netherlands to Russia, the Balkans, and northern Italy. There is also an isolated population in northern Spain. It inhabits damp situations, often at high altitudes, especially in the southern parts of its range. It requires a medium-sized aqua-terrarium with the temperature not exceeding 20°C (68°F), Feed on a variety of small invertebrates. Breeding habits are similar to other *Triturus* species.

Triturus cristatus (Great Crested or Warty Newt)—Length 17.5 cm (7 in). This is a relatively large, smart-looking newt in which both the male and the female develop a nuptial costume. The male in particular becomes a living rainbow; he develops a high, spiky crest which extends from just behind the head and

The Alpine Newt, *Triturus alpestris*, lives in moist woodland areas of central and eastern Europe.

The larval stage of the Great Crested Newt, *Triturus cristatus*, shown here, will last only about three months.

along the back to the start of the tail, where there is a deep indentation. The crest then re-emerges, but is less spiky along both the upper and lower edges of the broad, laterally flattened tail. The normally sooty-black body becomes light brown with dark blotches and a scattering of tiny white spots along the flanks. A light blue or whitish band develops toward the center of the tail. The belly color, which is retained throughout the year, is yellow to bright orange-red with black spots or blotches in both sexes. The female does not develop a crest, but the edges of her tail will widen in the breeding season. The Great Crested Newt occurs over much of central and northern Europe but in southwestern France and the Iberian peninsula it is replaced by *T. marmoratus*. Where the ranges of the two species overlap, hybrids of great beauty may occur. *T. cristatus* spends much of the year on land, but usually in moist situations.

In captivity it should have a large aqua-terrarium maintained at 20°C (68°F) in the summer. Temperature should be reduced to about 5 to 6°C (41 to 43°F) in the winter for a period of simulated hibernation. Feed on a

variety of small invertebrates. Breeds in the water in the earlier part of the year.

Triturus vittatus (Banded Newt)—Length 15 cm (6 in). The male Banded Newt in its nuptial costume must be the most spectacular of all newts, particularly the subspecies *T. v. ophryticus*. The ground color is reddish brown, covered with small dark spots. A broad, black-bordered, silvery white stripe extends along the flanks between the limbs, while the underside is yellow to orange. The breeding male has a deeply serrated crest that is as much as twice the depth of the body. The broad, flattened tail is also crested on both edges and is marked with blue and green blotches. This species occurs in southern Russia through southeastern Turkey to northern Iraq, Syria, Lebanon, and Israel, where it usually occurs in damp areas above 1000 meters (3250 ft). It requires a medium-sized aqua-terrarium with the temperature to 25°C (77°F) in summer, reduced in winter for a period of simulated hibernation. Feed on a variety of small invertebrates. The breeding habits are similar to those of *T. marmoratus*.

Notice how attractive the belly is on this Great Crested Newt, *Triturus cristatus*.

Although the One-toed Amphiuma, *Amphiuma pholeter*, can be kept in captivity, some keepers may be turned off by the fact that it is highly secretive and thus does not show itself often.

FAMILY AMPHIUMIDAE

One of the the smallest salamander families, with just a single genus and only three species, all of which are native to southeastern USA. They are totally aquatic and have internal gills with the openings just anterior to the forelimbs.

Amphiuma means (Two-toed Amphiuma)—Length 100 cm (39 in). This is probably the best known of the three amphiumas (the other two being *A. pholeter*, the One-toed, and *A. tridactylum*, the Three-toed). The Two-toed Amphiuma is a strongly built, eel-like salamander with four tiny limbs, each having only two digits.

It has very small, lidless eyes. It is uniform dark gray to brown above with a lighter gray underside. It is found in vegetated muddy waters, including swamps, bayous, and ditches, in the southeastern coastal plain of the USA from southeastern Virginia to Mississippi. Mainly nocturnal, it takes refuge in submerged burrows during the day. In moist weather conditions, it may migrate overland to another watercourse. It feeds on crayfish, frogs, other salamanders, fishes, and even small water snakes.

In captivity, it will do well in a large, well-aerated terrarium with a gravel substrate and larger rocks securely arranged to create hiding caves. Aquatic plants will soon be uprooted by the animals, so only floating plants should be used. The water temperature should be maintained at about 25°C (77°F) reduced to 18°C (65°F) in winter for a couple of months. Water must be chlorine-free and neutral to slightly acid (pH 6.8 to 7.0). Feed on tadpoles, small fishes, and pieces of lean meat or heart, etc. Amphiumas mate in the spring and fertilization is internal. The female seeks out a sheltered depression in the shallows where she lays about 200 eggs and remains coiled about them until they hatch (usually about 5 months later). The larvae are about 5 cm (2 in) long and, like most salamander larvae, have external gills. These are lost as they mature, leaving only a pair of gill slits.

FAMILY PROTEIDAE

Contains 6 species in 2 genera: *Necturus* with 5 species in eastern USA (mudpuppies and waterdogs), and *Proteus*, with a single species (the Olm, *Proteus anguinus*, a gilled, aquatic, cave-dwelling salamander which is rarely seen in captivity) in northeastern Italy and adjacent Slovenia.

Necturus maculosus (Mudpuppy)—Length 45 cm

Mudpuppies, *Necturus maculosus*, have always intrigued salamander hobbyists. They get their common name from the erroneous belief that they can actually bark.

(18 in) The largest and best known of the American proteid salamanders, the mudpuppy derives its English name from the erroneous belief that it can bark. In fact, the vocal talents of mudpuppies and waterdogs are confined to a feeble squeak. The mudpuppy is a robust, totally aquatic salamander with four four-toed limbs and a pair of dark red, feathery gills. It is gray-brown to dark gray above

cm (12 in). A layer of medium-grade gravel can be decorated with rocks and tree roots. Feed mudpuppies on small fishes, freshwater shrimps, water snails, and other aquatic animals. Breeding takes place in late spring, the female laying up to 200 eggs which she attaches to the underside of rocks, roots, or other debris. The hatchling larvae are about 2 cm (¾ in) long and can take up to 5 years to mature.

Although the Ringed Salamander, *Ambystoma annulatum*, would make a fine pet, it has a fairly limited natural range and is therefore rarely seen in the hobby.

with dark-edged bluish blotches; the underside is usually gray with darker markings. It is found in streams, rivers, and lakes in central and eastern USA. In captivity, mudpuppies require a large aquarium with filtered and aerated water to a depth of at least 30

FAMILY AMBYSTOMATIDAE
Contains 2 genera (*Ambystoma* and *Rhyacosiredon*) and 31 species distributed from southern Alaska and Canada through to the southern edge of the Mexican Plateau. The popular Axolotl, *Ambystoma mexicanum*, is

included in this family. The genus *Rhyacosiredon* has 4 species that are unlikely to be available to the terrarium keeper. Since they live in Mexican mountain streams, they require very specialized husbandry. In general, members of the genus *Ambystoma* are more suited for the terrarium.

Ambystoma annulatum (Ringed Salamander)—Length 20 cm (8 in). With a small head and a slender body, the Ringed Salamander is black to dark brown above with rings, bars, or patches of cream to yellow spaced from the head to the tail. The underside is gray, speckled with white. It is found in moist, forested areas from central Missouri southwest to western Arkansas and eastern Oklahoma. Secretive and burrowing in the wild, it is seen commonly only in the breeding season (October), when it mates in shallow pools. The eggs are attached to submerged vegetation. The larvae overwinter in the water and metamorphosis occurs in the following late spring. In captivity, a cool, moist aqua-terrarium is required. Feed on a variety of small invertebrates.

Ambystoma laterale (Blue-spotted Salamander)—Length 12.5 cm (5 in). A slender species with a narrow snout and short limbs. The color is

The Blue-spotted Salamander, *Ambystoma laterale*, is not a difficult caudate to maintain, but it is becoming rarer and rarer and is protected in some parts of its range.

blackish blue above with light blue spots and blotches, while the underside is grayish blue with darker blotching. It occurs throughout the Great Lakes region and extends to the Atlantic coast of North America. It

invertebrates. Mating occurs in ponds during March and April, and the female lays several batches of 10 to 15 eggs which are attached to aquatic vegetation or debris. Larvae hatch in about 30 days and these metamorphose to

Jefferson's Salamander, *Ambystoma jefferson-ianum*, was named after Jefferson College in southwestern Pennsylvania, which in turn was named after the third president of the United States, Thomas Jefferson.

mainly inhabits deciduous forest, where it burrows under ground litter, never far from permanent water.

It may be kept in a small aqua-terrarium containing a leaf-litter substrate. Humidity should be kept high, and summer temperatures of 15 to 20°C (59 to 68°F) are adequate. During the winter, keep at just above freezing (3 to 4°C— 37 to 39°F) for 2 or 3 months for simulated hibernation. It may be fed on a selection of small

terrestrial forms in 4 to 6 months.

Ambystoma jeffersonianum (Jefferson's Salamander)—Length 20 cm (8 in). Though this is a rather plain-looking species, it makes a rewarding terrarium inmate. Relatively long and slender, this species is dark brown to brownish gray above, occcasionally with bluish flecks on the limbs and lower flanks. It is found in deciduous forests in the northeastern

United States, where it usually burrows under surface debris near areas of permanent water. In captivity it requires a cool (15 to 20°C—59 to 68°F) aqua-terrarium. It may be fed on a variety of small invertebrates.

This species is known to hybridize with *A. laterale*, but the resulting offspring are all female.

Ambystoma maculatum (Spotted Salamander)— Length 25 cm (10 in). Spectacular in color and quite easy to keep, this species has come into great demand as a pet. It is one of the larger and more robust species in the family and has strong, well-developed limbs. It is bluish gray with two rows of large yellow or orange spots that start on top of the head and extend to the tail tip. It is usually a plain slate color beneath. In the wild, this species occurs throughout eastern North America from Nova Scotia and the Great Lakes almost to the Gulf Coast. It occurs mainly in areas of deciduous woodland, rarely far from permanent water. It lives in burrows during the day, but emerges at night or after heavy rains. Captive specimens require a large, woodland-type terrarium and access to

Some salamanders have to be provoked and even tricked into feeding, but not the Spotted Salamander, *Ambystoma maculatum*. This hardy little caudate is notorious for its voraciousness.

A dark and very private hidebox is a must for the Marbled Salamander, *Ambystoma opacum.* Although it will accept food regularly, it does not like being out in the open.

water for breeding. The humidity should be kept high, and the temperature should preferably not top 25°C (77°F). Feed on various small invertebrates including earthworms, slugs, and amphipods.

Ambystoma opacum (Marbled Salamander)— Length 12 cm (5 in). Though one of the smaller members of the genus, this species is quite robust in appearance. It is black, attractively marbled with steel-gray above, while the underside is plain black. It occurs in the eastern USA from the Great Lakes to the Gulf States, but not the Florida peninsula. It inhabits a variety of woodland sites, rarely far

from permanent water. However, mating occurs on land and the eggs are laid in damp depressions that later fill with rainwater. Until it rains, the female curls around and protects the eggs from desiccation. After hatching, the larvae transform into fully terrestrial forms in 4 to 6 months. In captivity it requires a medium-sized, humid terrarium with a summer temperature to 25°C (77°F). Reduce the temperature for a period of simulated hibernation in the winter.

Ambystoma tigrinum (Tiger Salamander)— Length 35 cm (14 in). This is probably the world's largest land-dwelling salamander species. A broad-headed, robust species, it makes a great subject for the salamander enthusiast and is usually in great demand. There are at least 6 subspecies with a huge variation in color and pattern. The ground color may be grayish, greenish, or brown, with whitish to yellowish stripes, patches, or marbling. It is very widespread across the USA from coast to coast and

salamanders are rarely seen during the daytime unless you are specifically searching them out by turning over forest litter or looking under and in decaying logs, etc. Breeding takes place in temporary pools, lakes, or streams in springtime, and the eggs are laid in masses attached to aquatic vegetation. Metamorphosis takes place in 5 to 6 months. Western populations may practice

An endangered species in many parts of its range, the Eastern Tiger Salamander, *Ambystoma tigrinum tigrinum*, was once a fairly common and reliable captive.

extends into Mexico. It occurs in varied habitats from damp woodland to fairly dry savannah. A secretive, burrowing species, wild tiger

neoteny, remaining in the water and eventually reaching 35 cm (14 in) in length. They are capable of reproducing in the larval form. Captive specimens

The Clouded Salamander, *Aneides ferreus*, is unusual because it can sometimes be found climbing in hollow trees and on shrubs.

require a large aqua-terrarium or aquarium for neotenous specimens. Provide a temperature range of 15 to 25°C (59 to 77°F), which can be further reduced in the winter. Feed them on a variety of invertebrates.

FAMILY PLETHODONTIDAE

This is the largest salamander family and contains two subfamilies (Desmognathinae with 3 genera and Plethodontinae with over 20 genera) with collectively over 220 species. Commonly known as "lungless salamanders" (they breathe through their

Central America to Brazil and Bolivia; two species, however, are found in southern Europe. Many new species have been described in recent years, most of these being from Mexico and Central America.

Aneides aeneus (Green Salamander)—Length 12 cm (5 in). This is an attractive little salamander that is marbled in black and glossy green to yellow-green along the back from the head to the tail tip. The limbs are usually reddish brown and the flanks and underside mottled

sensitive moist skin), the plethodontids occur primarily in the Americas from southern Alaska and Nova Scotia through

brownish. Due to its enormous jaw muscles, the rear part of the head appears to be swollen. In the USA, it ranges from

S.W. Pennsylvania through to central Alabama and North and South Carolina. It occurs in damp, hilly, forested areas, where it hides under logs or in rock crevices during the day and emerges at night to hunt small prey. It requires an unheated woodland type terrarium and should have a winter hibernation period. Like most lungless salamanders, it breeds on land. The eggs are laid in a secluded hollow and guarded by the female until they hatch. Full metamorphosis occurs in the egg, and hatchlings are miniature versions of adults.

Hydromantes italicus (Italian Cave Salamander)—Length 12 cm (5 in). This European plethodontid salamander is reddish brown in color with a marbling of yellowish to pinkish. The underside is usually darkly colored with whitish marbling. This species occurs in extreme S.E. France across northern Italy and extending to central Italy on the eastern half of the peninsula. It lives in moist, rocky situations under stones, logs, etc. It is nocturnal and retreats deep into crevices during long periods of dry weather. In captivity it requires a moist terrarium provided

The genus *Aneides* is known collectively as the climbing salamanders, and rightly so. Members of the genus are among the most arboreal salamanders in the world. Shown is the Black Salamander, *Aneides flavi-punctatus*.

with rocks and ferns. Maintain summer daytime temperature at 25°C, reducing to 15°C at night. Winter temperature range 10 to 20°C. Feed on a variety of small invertebrates. Breeding habits are similar to *Aneides aeneus*.

sea level to 1600 meters (5200 ft). During the day it takes refuge under rocks and fallen timber, emerging at night to forage for food. As its skin secretes a sticky substance which is difficult to remove, it should be handled with care!

It requires a medium-

Slimy Salaman- ders, *Plethodon glutinosus* and their close allies, are very widespread, covering much of the eastern United States.

Plethodon glutinosus (Slimy Salamander)— Length 20 cm (8 in). A slender, elongate species with a round body and a flattened head, it is mainly black with cream or white spots concentrated along the flanks. Beneath it is slate blue, often mottled with white. Its natural range is the eastern USA and into southeastern Canada. It is found in a range of habitats from near

sized, cool terrarium with a gravel and leaf-litter substrate and a few flat stones and plants. Provide a period of simulated hibernation in the winter. Breeding is similar to *A. aeneus*.

Pseudotriton ruber (Red Salamander)—Length 18 cm (7 in). This is one of the most attractively colored North American salamanders and is much-prized by terrarium keepers. There are 4 subspecies, and colors range from bright orange-red to purplish above, with numerous small black spots. The underside is pinkish and may be spotted with black. Found in the eastern USA except the southeastern coastal plain and most of Florida, it occurs in very damp habitats, particularly around springs and seepages to altitudes of 1500 meters (4875 ft). It is noturnal, hiding under cover during the day. It requires a large terrarium

Unlike most other plethodontids, the Red Salamander lays its eggs in shallow water and these hatch into larvae which may take over 2 years to transform.

FAMILY SIRENIDAE

Contains two genera (*Siren* and *Pseudobranchus*) with respectively two and one species, all native to North America.

Siren lacertina (Greater Siren)—Length: 97 cm (38 in). Perhaps some of the most fascinating of all salamanders, these

Eel-like in appearance, the Greater Siren, *Siren lacertina*, has no hind legs and can be found most often in fairly shallow water.

with a high humidity. A gravel substrate and mossy rocks will provide the furnishing. Try and provide an artificial drip seepage.

remarkable amphibians have no hind limbs, tiny forelimbs, and an eel-like body. As its name implies, the largest member of the

Not too much is known about the life history of the Narrow-striped Dwarf Siren, *Pseudobranchus striatus axanthus*. The subspecies wasn't even described until the early 1940's.

the family is the Greater Siren. It has a stout, eel-like body that is gray to olive above, occasionally with darker spots. The flanks are paler in color, with many faint yellowish blotches. It has three pairs of feathery external gills. The flat tail is rounded at the tip. The Greater Siren is a native of the coastal plain of the southeastern USA from the District of Columbia to Florida and Alabama, where it inhabits shallow, muddy, highly

vegetated waters. The breeding habits of sirens are poorly documented, but the female lays her eggs on the roots and foliage of water plants. In captivity it requires a large aquarium with a deep substrate (fine gravel or sand) and a water depth of about 35 cm (14 in). Maintain temperature at about to 25°C (77°F), but reduce to 16 to 18°C (60 to 65°F) in winter. Feed on small fish, snails, crustaceans, insect larvae, and aquatic plants.

Suggested Reading

TFH has produced more books on the care of salamanders and newts than any other publisher in the world. You can find them in pet shops the world over.

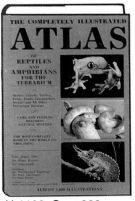

H-1102, Over 800 pages, over 1,800 Illustrations

TS-182, Over 190 pages, over 175 full-color photos

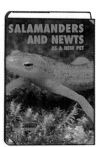

TU-023, Over 60 pages, over 50 full-color photos

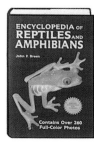

H-935, Over 550 pages, over 260 full-color photos

PS-876, Over 350 pages, over 175 full-color photos

Photo Index

Alpine Newt, 47, 81
Ambystoma annulatum, 86
Ambystoma cingulatum, 34, 59
Ambystoma gracile, 26–27
Ambystoma jeffersonianum, 88
Ambystoma laterale, 87
Ambystoma macrodactylum, 49, 63
Ambystoma maculatum, 33, 89
Ambystoma mexicanum, 67, 71
Ambystoma opacum, 90
Ambystoma tigrinum californiense, 6, 69
Ambystoma tigrinum tigrinum, 55, 91
Amphiuma pholeter, 84
Aneides ferreus, 92
Aneides flavipunctatus, 5, 93
Axolotl, 67, 71
Batrachoseps attenuatus, 68
Black Salamander, 5, 93
Black-spotted Newt, 15
Blue-spotted Salamander, 87

Bolitoglossa altamazonica, 13, 57
Bolitoglossa subpalmata, 10, 37
Broken-striped Newt, 35
California Newt, 60
California Slender Salamander, 68
California Tiger Salamander, 6, 69
Clouded Salamander, 92
Cryptobranchus alleganiensis, 74
Cryptobranchus alleganiensis bishopi, 73
Cryptobranchus sp., 11
Cynops ensicauda, 8, 9
Cynops ensicauda popei, 18–19
Desmognathus ochrophaeus, 31
Eastern Newt, 37
Eastern Red-spotted Newt, 76–77
Eastern Tiger Salamander, 55, 91
Eastern Zigzag Salamander, 17
Ensatina, 12, 24, 53, 65
Ensatina eschscholtzi, 53, 65
Ensatina eschscholtzi klauberi, 7, 36

Ensatina sp., 12, 24
Eurycea longicauda guttolineata, 62
Fire Salamander, 30, 80
Flatwoods Salamander, 34, 59
Georgia Blind Salamander, 41
Great Crested Newt, 82, 83
Greater Siren, 16, 95
Gyrinophilus palleucus, 29
Gyrinophilus porphyriticus, 21, 40
Haideotriton wallacei, 410
Hellbender, 11, 74
Hong Kong Newt, 75
Jefferson's Salamander, 88
Jordan's Salamander, 56
Large-blotched Salamander, 7, 36
Long-toed Salamander, 49, 63
Marbled Newt, 20
Marbled Salamander, 90
Mountain Dusky Salamander, 31
Mudpuppy, 85
Narrow-striped Dwarf Siren, 96
Necturus maculosus, 85
Northwestern Salamander, 26–27
Notophthalmus meridionalis, 15
Notophthalmus viridescens, 37, 39, 76–77
Notophthalmus viridescens dorsalis, 35
One-toed Amphiuma, 84
Ozark Hellbender, 73
Paramesotriton hongkongensis, 75
Plethodon dorsalis dorsalis, 17
Plethodon glutinosus, 94
Plethodon jordani, 56
Pleurodeles waltl, 61, 72, 78
Pseudobranchus striatus axanthus, 96
Pseudoeurycea belli, 49
Pseudoeurycea gigantea, 22
Red Eft, 39
Ringed Salamander, 86
Rough-skinned Newt, 79
Salamandra salamandra, 30, 80
Siren lacertina, 16, 95
Slimy Salamander, 94
Spanish Ribbed Newt, 61, 72, 78
Spotted Salamander, 33, 89
Spring Salamander, 21, 40
Swordtail Newt, 8, 9
Taricha granulosa, 79
Taricha torosa, 60
Tennessee Cave Salamander, 29
Three-lined Salamander, 62
Triturus alpestris, 47, 81
Triturus cristatus, 82, 83
Triturus marmoratus, 20

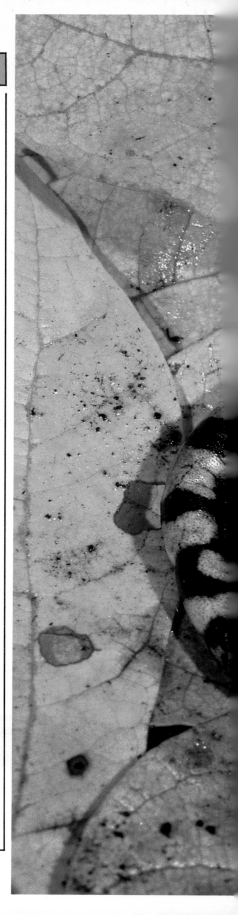